ALSO BY H. E. BATES

Novels

THE TWO SISTERS
CHARLOTTE'S ROW
THE POACHER
SPELLA HO
THE CRUISE OF THE BREADWINNER
THE JACARANDA TREE
LOVE FOR LYDIA
THE SLEEPLESS MOON
THE DARLING BUDS OF MAY
A BREATH OF FRENCH AIR
A CROWN OF WILD MYRTLE
THE DISTANT HORNS OF SUMMER

CATHERINE FOSTER
THE FALLOW LAND
A HOUSE OF WOMEN
FAIR STOOD THE WIND FOR FRANCE
THE PURPLE PLAIN
THE SCARLET SWORD
THE FEAST OF JULY
WHEN THE GREEN WOODS LAUGH
THE DAY OF THE TORTOISE
OH! TO BE IN ENGLAND
A MOMENT IN TIME
A LITTLE OF WHAT YOU FANCY

THE TRIPLE ECHO (*Illustrated by Ron Clarke*)

Short Stories

DAY'S END
THE BLACK BOXER
CUT AND COME AGAIN
THE FLYING COAT
THE BRIDE COMES TO EVENSFORD
COLONEL JULIAN
THE WATERCRESS GIRL
DEATH OF A HUNTSMAN
THE GOLDEN ORIOLE
THE WILD CHERRY TREE
SEVEN TAILS OF ALEXANDER

THE WOMAN WHO HAD
  IMAGINATION
SOMETHING SHORT AND SWEET
THE BEAUTY OF THE DEAD
DEAR LIFE
THE DAFFODIL SKY
NOW SLEEPS THE CRIMSON PETAL
THE NATURE OF LOVE
AN ASPIDISTRA IN BABYLON
THE FOUR BEAUTIES
THE SONG OF THE WREN

Drama

THE DAY OF GLORY

Essays

FLOWERS AND FACES
DOWN THE RIVER
THE HEART OF THE COUNTRY
THE COUNTRY HEART

THROUGH THE WOODS
THE SEASONS AND THE GARDENER
O! MORE THAN HAPPY COUNTRYMAN
THE COUNTRY OF WHITE CLOVER

EDWARD GARNETT: A MEMOIR

Collections of Short Stories

THIRTY TALES

THE FABULOUS MRS V.
COUNTRY TALES
MY UNCLE SILAS
(*Illustrated by Edward Ardizzone*)

THE WEDDING PARTY
SEVEN BY FIVE
SUGAR FOR THE HORSE
(*Illustrated by Edward Ardizzone*)

Criticism

THE MODERN SHORT STORY

Autobiography

THE VANISHED WORLD
(*Illustrated by John Ward*)

THE BLOSSOMING WORLD
(*Illustrated by John Ward*)

THE WORLD IN RIPENESS (*Illustrated by John Ward*)

As 'Flying Officer X'

THE GREATEST PEOPLE IN THE WORLD

HOW SLEEP THE BRAVE

For Children

ACHILLES THE DONKEY

ACHILLES AND DIANA

Gardening

A LOVE OF FLOWERS (*Illustrated by Pauline Ellison*)

60p

A Fountain of Flowers

A Fountain of Flowers

H. E. BATES

Colour Plates by Patrick Matthews

MICHAEL JOSEPH

First published in Great Britain by MICHAEL JOSEPH LTD
52 Bedford Square London WC1

1974

© Evensford Productions 1974

ISBN 0 7181 1158 3

Printed in Great Britain by
Redwood Burn Limited
Trowbridge and Esher
and bound by Dorstel Press, Harlow

Preface

The man is the book; the book is the man. This incontestable truth, which I often repeat to myself, I claim to be as true of gardens as it is of authors and their books. As a man is, so is his garden. He is a reflection of it, and it of him.

For this reason, whenever I am asked how I planned my garden, I always reply "I didn't. It evolved." Moreover it evolved from a very unpromising piece of a farmyard full of docks, nettles, thistles and just about every other noxious weed common to farmyards. Moreover – and this a point of much importance – it is still evolving. A garden, as I have said before, should never stand still. It should never be a monument to complacency. However beautiful it may be, there is surely, always, something that isn't quite right – a path needs widening here, a border there needs to be narrowed, a bed elsewhere needs a deeper, more flowing curve, a section of the rock garden has become so overgrown that it looks like a man with too long a beard, the bones of it, or the rocks, invisible under forests of plant whiskers.

Whenever these things occur, or others of the same kind, I bring out a ruthless hand. Change, I tell myself, is not decay; change is resuscitation, a new view, excitement. So, every year, some part of the garden, however small, is torn apart and remoulded nearer to the heart's desire.

Those silly flag irises that flower for a bare fortnight in midsummer – what *are* they doing there? taking up precious space that could be filled with something that would flower three or four months, such as that glorious purple beauty, *Aster frikartii,* which will give you joy from July to November. And why persist with that indifferent lump of lupins, that flake away in a week of hot sun, when they could be replaced by something such as *Artemisia* 'Lambrooke Silver', a flowerless grey of pure loveliness that will light up the border with incomparable incandescence and at the same time cool down the autumn fires of dahlias, or that other incomparable delight *Sedum* 'Autumn Joy', so exquisite in green bud, still more exquisite in its green-and-claret half-open flower, and most exquisite of all in its rich full red wine vintage, a dancing stage for butterflies for weeks on end.

All this pre-supposes a considerable knowledge of plants, often very uncommon ones, that can only come of long and wide experience. But are knowledge and experience enough? Are they everything? I contend not. Something of infinitely greater importance is needed before one can achieve the ultimate state where it can be said "the man is the garden, the garden the man". And this something, I maintain, is affection.

Last summer a well-known horticulturist and writer on gardening matters, who himself owns a garden of classical grace conforming to the highest possible standards, asked if he could come to see my garden. I said yes and trembled. What on earth could an old bungling amateur like me have to offer that could possibly interest the trained and knowledgeable professional? I feared a keen and critical eye.

I needn't have worried. It happened that he arrived on an evening of delicious autumn light falling at a low angle on the garden in its full late glory. Great purple stretches of

10

Verbena rigida (*venosa*), another treasure that will flower for six months; an aristocrat among fuchsias, the red-leaved, orange-flowered *Thalia;* the silky mauve carpet of *Convolvulus mauritanicus;* the pink and scarlet glory of two salvias, *S. involucratta* and *S. fulgens* – all this, together with an array of many green-and-gold variegations of foliage, served to set the evening in tune, so that if the flowers didn't actually sing they appeared to be in symphonic harmony.

Next day the bungling old amateur received a gracious letter from the experienced professional.

"I loved your garden," he wrote, "because it gave the feeling of being loved."

My garden, in fact, was I; it wasn't professionally designed by one of those firms of landscape gardeners whose work you see every year at Chelsea. It was conceived in love, was loved and gave the feeling of being loved.

That, in fact, is what true gardens are made of. Not wholly of professional skills or tomes of encyclopaedic knowledge or even of green fingers: but love.

[1]

Quite the most fascinating thing about gardening, to my mind, is that it is an endless voyage of discovery. Constantly you are coming upon a plant of which, though it may have been in cultivation for a couple of centuries, you have never heard before. Recently I was glancing through that famous book Thornton's *Temple of Flora*, first published in 1807. This book, as Mr Geoffrey Grigson points out in his preface to a new edition of it, is really not of any great appeal to 'the botanical scientist or even to the scientific or painstaking gardener'; it is simply 'an extraordinary theatre of romanticism.'

Theatre is right; the plants and flowers depicted in it are like theatrical characters, some gaudy, some lovable, some enchanting, some mysterious, some villainous, some sinister, some poisonous, some having a strange quality of surrealism. Next to a plate of picottee carnations and old-fashioned 'broken' tulips (which, happily, you can still buy), you find a creature called the Maggot-bearing Stapelia, which looks rather like a dark, sinister octopus that has somehow got a football rosette stuck on to it – quite one of the oddest characters you ever saw.

And what on earth is a China Limodorum? An Orchid of South East Asia, it looks like some exotic architectural hyacinth and rather like a sister of another oddity, this time from North East India and Burma, called the 'Nodding

12

Renealmia'. Side by side with these two not unbeautiful curiosities is a common villain, the dirtiest scoundrel ever, at once to be hissed off the stage – the Dragon Arum (*Dracunculus vulgaris*) with its noxious purple spathe and its even more noxious stink which is an overpowering combination of a charnel house and an open sewer. This horror, which should never, never be planted in a garden (I know, because I once unwisely planted it in mine) would seem to be rivalled, if that is possible, by an American bog plant aptly named the Skunk Cabbage.

But not all, thank goodness, is romantic horror. Three enchanting passion flowers are depicted, the Blue Passion Flower, well known of course and in cultivation since the 17th century, the Winged Passion Flower and the Quadrangular Passion Flower. Of these last two I have had no experience; nor until recently had I any idea that there were also a pink passion flower and a wine-red one, two charming climbers of which you can get seed. *Passiflora quadrangularis* is otherwise known as the Grenadilla, having pink flowers and blue, red purple fruits which are edible.

Another recent discovery of mine and quite one of the most ethereal things I ever saw is *Petrea* sometimes known as Purple Wreath. This is also a climber and can best be described, I think, as an infinitely refined wisteria, not the least lovely feature about it being a darker central petal, looking like a piece of purple velvet sewn on as an after-thought by some meticulous seamstress. I fear, however, that it isn't hardy here, though I fancy the cool house would afford it protection enough. Just as lovely is *Allamanda cathartica*, with its shiny rich green leaves and butter-golden trumpets that look as if they were moulded from wax. This needs considerable warmth, so that putting it into a cool house will only court failure.

The same is true of *Stephanotis*, whose exquisite pure white trumpets, rich with heavenly perfume, grace endless brides' bouquets year in, year out. But if you can't grow this you can always try *Jasminum polyanthum*, its narrower white trumpets, at first rich pink in the bud, being just as exquisitely scented. This, so nearly hardy, presents no trouble, strikes easily from cuttings and can be trained into conical pyramids which are quite excellent in the house. An equally beautiful climber is *Hoya carnosa*, with thick leathery leaves and pendant clusters of waxy pink flowers, also richly scented, each of which carries, every morning, a globule of honey-tasting nectar at the tip. And speaking of tips, here is a tip about the *Hoya*. Never over-pot it. My own plant, now ten years old, still lives happily and profitably in its original six-inch pot and obliges by flowering twice or even three times a year, whereas many cuttings given away to friends and constantly re-potted have never flowered at all.

Lastly a plant entirely new to me but one of much enchantment: *Iboza riparia*, formerly *Moschosma riparia*. This graceful plant with its delicate sprays of lilac-pink flowers comes, I think, from Rhodesia. Its winter requirements under glass are not, apparently, exacting; it also strikes easily from cuttings and I am therefore hoping to use it rather as I use two excellent salvias, *S. fulgens* and *S. involucrata*, planting it out in summer and then securing cuttings before winter sets in. To me it looks like a very desirable thing.

[2]

2.   I recently came across two well-known writers on gardening matters separately pursuing the same fallacy about the classical names of plants. Both were making a plea for the use, wherever possible, of Latin names in addition to common names, especially in catalogues, so that as one writer put it, "the customer can really know what he is buying".

This immediately sent me on a small but very rewarding voyage of discovery, some results of which I will now proceed to examine so that perhaps, when you next pick up a catalogue, you too will have some idea of what you are buying. Perhaps it would be more correct to say that the voyage wasn't so much one of discovery as one of confirmation, since I was already convinced in my own mind that the notion that classical names are automatically Latin names was very, very wide of the truth. And so, in fact, it turned out to be.

Delphinium, dianthus, crocus, narcissus, lithospermum, jasminum, hyacinthus, hypericum, thalictrum – here, you might well say, is a strong string of Latin-looking names, all of which you could find in any comprehensive catalogue. In fact none of them is pure Latin. One is Arabic, one, verbena, is Celtic. The rest are Greek.

Thus *delphinium* is from the Greek *delphis*, a *dolphin*; *dianthus* from the Greek *dius*, God, *anthos*, flower – that is

15

to say the divine flower; *crocus* is from the Greek *Krokos*, saffron, an ingredient we all know; *narcissus* is from the Greek *narkissos*, deriving from *narkao*, to stupefy, some bulbs of the genus apparently having the power to do just that, a fact that most of us probably didn't know; *lithospermum*, looking as Latin as Augustus Caesar, is nevertheless from the Greek *lithos*, a stone, and *sperma*, a seed; *hyacinthus* is from the Greek *hyakinthos*, a Spartan youth killed by Apollo; *hypericum* is from the Greek *hyper*, over, and *ereika*, a heath; *linaria* is from the Greek *linon*, flax, hence the common name, 'toad-flax' for one of the species; *thalictrum* is from the Greek *thallo*, to become green. The only other non-Latin runner is *jasminum*, said to come from the Arabic name for jasmine, *ysmyn*.

This is not to say that either Greek or Latin, or both, have virtually a monopoly of plant names. *Tulipa* probably derives from the Turkish word *tulbana*, a turban, which refers to the shape of the flower; *salix* is from the Celtic *sal*, near, and *lis*, water; *Rosa* is Celtic again, from *rhod*, meaning red; *doronicum* is from the Arabic *doronigi*.

Very many plant names, however, are commemorative and derive from no particular language, being either named after botanists of distinction or plant collectors who first discovered them. Thus *tradescantia* is named after John Tradescant, gardener to Charles the First, who with his son discovered and introduced to cultivation a vast number of plants; *davidia* owes its name to the French missionary Père David; *lobelia* is named in commemoration of Mathew Lobel, physician to James the First; *aubrieta* honours a French botanist, M. Aubriet, and *begonia* another French botanist, M. Bégon; fuchsia is named after Dr. Fuchs, a German botanist, *funkia* after another German one, Dr. Funk; *camellia*, which gives us not only those glorious red, white and pink rosettes of such chaste perfection but also, of course, tea, is named after a Moravian Jesuit.

16

Nor do the origins of plant names end here. Often they derive from the shape of the flower. The flowers of *digitalis* are like fingers, or digits, hence the common name foxgloves; *helenium* is named after Helen of Troy, the flowers having been said to have sprung from her tears; Gentius, a king of Illyria, gives his name to the gentians; papaver is possibly from *papa*, thick milk, referring to the thick juice of the poppy; *iberis* is from the old name for Spain, Iberia; legend says that *daphne* is named after Daphne who, pursued by Apollo, was rescued by being turned into a spurge laurel, which is the plant's common name; *cydonia*, is from an old name for a quince which grew at Cydon in Crete; *yucca* is simply from the native Peruvian name. Some derivations are obscure and controversial, one of these being *veronica*, which may refer to St Veronica's sacred handkerchief, or may mean truly unique, or derive from Vatonica, an ancient Roman name for a Spanish province.

No, it's by no means all Latin or even all Greek, though I would be prepared to bet that Greek wins by two to one.

And one day I shall explore a further field, finding out for myself why certain common plant names are the same in various languages – i.e. forget-me-not in English, *ne m'oubliez pas* in French, pansy in English, *pensée* in French. As to the vernacular names for dandelion in English, French and German – well, I won't go into that just now.

[3]

There are some families of plants – salvias and euphorbias being good examples – which have far too many children, so that it is impossible to know or enjoy more than a tiny fraction of them. Others have all too few. I am thinking now of the abutilons, which number among their cousins the mallows, the hollyhocks and the so called tree-hollyhock or hibiscus (*Hibiscus syriacus*).

Unfortunately the abutilons are not hardy, most of them coming from South America, but in the case of two of them, *A. megapotamicum* and *A. vitifolium*, this need be no deterrent, since both are readily raised from cuttings or seed. (A very nice Mrs Malaprop I know said the other day that she thought prison was a good detergent – which is a very good near bull's eye if you think of it.) I have sung the praises of *A. megapotamicum* before and have tried to describe it, though perhaps not very successfully. (The megapotamicum bit means, it would seem, 'from the great river'.) This lovely thing has delicate pendant flowers in red, yellow and black, so that I sometimes think of them as exotic fuchsias or better, perhaps as Chinese lanterns. It will make a thin loose shrub of up to six feet and I have known it to thrive outside on a wall, where it will flower profusely all summer. A safer method with it, I find, is to keep it in a large pot and plunge it outside from June to October. Cuttings taken in spring will flower very quickly and in a cool house may well go on flowering into and even through the winter.

A. vitifolium describes itself, since the leaves are vine-shaped, as in fact they are in *A. megapotamicum*. Here I must qualify my remarks about hardiness by saying that my own *vitifolium* (which has now died of old age) survived the bitter winters of 1940 and 1947 and even survived a transplant when it couldn't have been less than fifteen years old. It was also generous with seed. Its flowers, which marry beautifully with the grey-green vine-shaped foliage, are slightly floppy and of the purest, softest mauve. There is also a white variety and I have also heard of a double or semi-double version, which I have never seen. Altogether it is a highly desirable and beautiful thing.

Vine-shaped too are the leaves of *A. darwinii*, from which most of the commonly seen hybrids in yellow, rose, orange and red derive. These have the added charm of delicious mottlings and marblings, mostly in gold and green, on the leaves, which in consequence are rather more to be desired than the flowers. Most good seed catalogues list these hybrids which, if sown under glass early in the year, will start to flower by the end of July, though, as I say, the lovely variegation of leaf makes the flowering a matter of less importance, more especially as the flowers, which are again rather like Chinese lanterns, are not very long lasting.

The habits of old professional gardeners die hard; and for the life of me I can never understand why this *Abutilon* is for ever used as what is repulsively called 'a dot plant'. Look into any public park in summer and there you will see it, stuck about in formal beds of geraniums, alyssum, lobelia and such things, like an unfortunate afterthought. The whole thing is an insult to a plant so beautiful in itself that its rightful place is surely either on its own or grouped with other shrubs or sub-shrubs for contrasting effect of foliage. Since it will grow up to six feet high it is surely worth a separate place of honour. It will also do splendidly in the

19

greenhouse and will make an extremely striking and easy room plant too. Both seed and cuttings are child's play.

There is no need here to say anything of hollyhocks, since everyone knows them so well, but the tree mallows *Lavatera arborea*, having purple flowers, and *L. olbia*, with soft pink flowers are, I rather think, not very well known. Here again the leaves are vine-shaped. *L. arborea* is the less hardy of the two and though a hard winter will knock *L. olbia* about a bit it usually recovers quickly if pruned back in spring and is anyway so prodigal with seed that its progeny may even become a slight embarrassment. A good sub-shrub, this, with its pale grey leaves, to light up the back of a big border.

The hibiscus I am now writing about mustn't be confused with the hibiscus of the tropics, of which there are species other than those that provide Polynesian maidens with those magnificently inviting blossoms which they stick into the side of their blue-black hair. (Speaking of Polynesian girls, you can dismiss from your mind the idea that their grass skirts are made of grass. They are in fact made from the bark of one of the tropical hibiscus, which also has flowers having the fascinating habit of changing colour from pale cream in the morning to deep red at night, when they fall from the tree, their daily conjuring act finished.)

No: the hibiscus to which I now refer are of *Hibiscus syriacus* with mallow-like flowers of blue, pink, red, white, violet, both single and double, and in several cases with prettily blotched petals. These shrubs are quite hardy, neat in habit and need little or no pruning. But perhaps their greatest virtue is the lateness of their flowering. August, September and even October are the months when they come into their own and where their highly attractive blossoms are consequently doubly precious. They are not at all unlike the tropical hibiscus, though much smaller, and I suppose you can, if you wish, wear them in your hair to indicate, as Polynesian girls do, whether you are fancy-free or not. Unfortunately I can't remember whether you wear them on the right hand side for "Come hither" or the left hand side for "off off!" Not that I think Polynesian girls are very particular about such matters. They are noted for being very free with their charms.

[4]

On a beautiful July day in the glorious summer of 1970, in one of Kent's loveliest and most celebrated villages, I suddenly came upon a riotous assembly. No: not of drug addicts, raving students, protesting Pakistanis, opponents of apartheid or anything of that sort, but simply a riotous assembly of annuals, in a modest cottage garden. Unplanned, unprofessional, uninhibited, it was a blazing kaleidoscope of scarlet, purple, pink, orange, white, yellow and just about every other colour you care to think of. Salvias, petunias, snapdragons, fuchsias, stocks, sweet peas, marigolds, nasturtiums and much else: all had been planted by a prodigal hand, haphazard, colour clashing against colour, so that no single inch of earth could be seen. And the total effect, which ought by all the rules to have been vulgar, was somehow right, rich and delightful.

After that first view I suppose I saw this example of riotous assembly every week from July until the November woods glowed on the hillsides above the village in a magnificence of burnished gold and copper. By that time, in a long mild spell, asters, dahlias and chrysanthemums had added a little more riot to the assembly, so that the autumnal richness was even wilder than that of summer had been.

I was so fascinated by all this that if it hadn't been for one fact I might well have been tempted to plan, for 1971,

22

a riotous assembly of my own. The one fact was, however, that I had already done so. In one part of my garden – it was once the stable-yard – I have five formal oblong beds, edged with York stone, that form a cross. In spring these are always pretty with tulips, mostly the lily-flowered varieties, and a particularly good dark blue forget-me-not. In summer they have generally been planted with fuchsias and *Verbena rigida* (*V. venosa*), but the splendid summer of 1969, though suiting so many things very well, proved altogether too dry for fuchsias and the whole plan was, also, a near-failure.

It was to prevent this happening again that I decided to experiment with my own form of riotous assembly. By planting twenty different things, instead of two, I ought to be able, I reasoned, to insure myself against whatever kind of summer might prevail. Nor, I also reasoned, would there be only flowers; I would take out a second insurance with foliage.

Accordingly I settled not only for my favourite *Verbena rigida* and some fuchsias, which I cannot bear to be without, but also fibrous begonias, gloriosa daisies (what marvellous value these rudbeckias are, blooming as they do for the better part of six months; I will never be without them;) *Convolvulus tricolor*, most lovable in its purple, white and gold, *Nicotiana* 'Lime Green', *Dimorphotheca* or *Osteospermun eklonis*, (I call it the government flower because it opens at 9 in the morning and shuts at 4 in the afternoon), the gentian-blue *Salvia patens*, *Phlox drummondii* and some geraniums. The geraniums were, however, part of the foliage insurance scheme. With their delightful variegations of leaf in silver and green, gold and green, and pink and green, they would give pleasure whether the summer was wet or fine. As it was, the summer was glorious and to the leaf variegations were added a brilliance of rose and cherry flowers.

23

The foliage insurance scheme was also responsible for the silver-leaved gazanias, the silver feathers of *Pyrethrum ptarmiciflorum*, and coleus. At this point, I am sure, the purists will start mumbling into their beards. Let them mumble. I am very fond of coleus and I see no reason why they shouldn't be part of an outdoor riotous assembly. They are very lovely if used informally. Another part of the foliage insurance scheme might well have come from *Lobelia cardinalis*, with its grenadier-scarlet flowers and coppery-red leaves, or those dwarfer dahlias with the same leaf-and-flower combination of colour. As it happened, I had none of these to spare.

One plant, however, strayed into the scheme not by design but by accident. For most of the summer it remained a mystery. Having been a gift in the first place, it had no name. It looked like a hydrangea of sorts but clearly wasn't. It also looked like part of the foliage insurance scheme, with its handsome tongue-like leaves with rich dark veins. But would it flower? July, August and the first week of September brought no answer. Then buds appeared and in due course opened: sprigs of pink and white coral, delicate and entrancing.

At this point the detective in me got to work. The plant, I had been telling myself for some time past, was surely a polygonum, one of the knot-weeds (docks, if you must know) and so it proved. A little investigation showed it to be *Polygonum campanulatum* and it is, I assure you, well worth making a note of.

So my riotous assembly was a success too, flowering on and on, as it did, until the end of November. It also proved what I had suspected when I first came upon the cottage garden riot in July. It isn't by always following the rules that, in gardening, you necessarily get the best results. In other words you can have, for my money, fifty gardens planned by experts from Chelsea in exchange for one

General View of H. E. Bates' garden in the spring

General view. The welter of colour that H. E. Bates enjoyed

Sissinghurst. *Wisteria floribunda* 'Alba'

Helleborus lividus corsicus and white tulips

coat-of-many-colours scheme unplanned by a cottager on the south slopes of the Kentish hills. Experts, of course have their uses; but now and then it's nice to be a little dizzy for a change.

[5]

A correspondent, a friend of that celebrated gardener, the late Margery Fish, recently sent me a list of certain plants from her Cornish garden, adding that if I cared to have plants or cuttings of them she would be delighted to send them. I thanked her for her generous thought, saying that I should be delighted to receive her gift but adding that I was ashamed to have to confess that I had never heard of the plants she named.

"No need to be ashamed," she wrote back and went on to name two distinguished horticulturists who had never heard of them either, the reason being that most of the plants were not in commerce. Nor could I find them in any of my many books on gardening. Some had come from gardens in Cornwall, others from old Irish gardens. *Vestia lycioides* was one which eluded me completely; *Berberis darlergensis* 'Pink Pearls' was another.

When the plants and cuttings finally arrived they were accompanied by a note in which my correspondent confessed to being "slightly batty about variegated things". This pleased me, since I am slightly batty about variegated things myself. I was even more pleased to find that the parcel of plants and cuttings contained a lot of variegated things I didn't possess, among them a deep golden ivy from Tralee, a variegated Portugal laurel, a variegated *laurustinus*, a variegated *Hydrangea*, a variegated London Pride, a silver privet and a *Weigela* of a different variegation from the one I already possessed.

All this prompted me to do a little tour of investigation in my own garden, just to see what number of variegations it did contain. I was surprised and delighted to find that it had far more than I had supposed. Undoubtedly the queen of them all was *Eleagnus pungens aurea maculata*, which with its brilliant gold-and-green leaves is the most lovely and luminous of things, magnificently alight, especially in winter. This indispensable beauty is never a very large shrub, but it utterly dwarfs a real miniature poppet, of which I am very fond, called *Hypericum × moserianum* 'tricolor', an almost prostrate Rose of Sharon with pink, green and gold leaves and little yellow flowers of much refinement. (My Cornish correspondent had, by the way, included cuttings of another *Eleagnus, fredericii*, of slightly paler gold than *pungens aurea*.)

It was now getting slightly late in the year for *Phlox paniculata* 'Norah Leigh', a very worthwhile thing treasured for its cream-and-green foliage rather than its washy pink flowers; but two variegated periwinkles, one with large leaves and large mauve flowers and the other correspondingly smaller in every way, were still flourishing happily. So were a gold-green fuchsia, the name of which I have unfortunately lost, and a gold-green *Hebe*, still bearing its bright purple bottle-brush flowers. This is *× andersonii* 'Variegata' – not reliably hardy but so easy from cuttings that it can be saved without difficulty in a cold house or frame.

Another favourite charmer of mine, the variegated form of *Fuchsia magellanica gracilis*, is quite hardy if its pruning (to ground level) is left until spring. Not at all hardy, of course, are the many variegated geraniums. Another plant I both like and admire and which, alas, is cursed with an undeserved reputation born of suburban gardens and chapel yards, is the variegated laurel. It too, with its brilliant green-and-gold, brings a lovely touch of illumination to shady and/or wintry places. The same is true of the excellent variegated hollies and yet another shrub cursed with a bad reputation, our much misused friend the golden privet, which even that great gardener Gertrude Jekyll didn't despise. She, on the contrary, used it in her borders with great effect. Another good small shrub not often seen is the variegated snowberry, which has the misfortune to bear the name *Symphoricarpos orbiculatus* 'Variegatus', an affliction it certainly doesn't deserve.

I think I have now grown most of the variegated hostas, both silver and gold, and very charming they are, but it was only recently that I acquired a gold-and-green sedum, which has a cool and tranquillising effect. A nice obliging little miniature is a silver thyme, which looks well in light shade. *Euonymus forturei* 'Silver Queen' will also tolerate shade, even quite deep shade, and its green-and-silver leaves provide further charm by being slightly touched with pink in winter. It makes excellent ground cover too. Two maples are worthy of a good place, especially in front of a very dark green conifer or yew – *Acer negundo* 'Variegatum' and *A. platanoides* 'Drummondii'. And lastly a variegated *Bergenia*. This I have seen in Madeira, which makes me suspect it may not be hardy here. But I am still searching for it and perhaps one day I may be lucky.

[6]

Are you fond of wine? or does your taste for it need to be stimulated? If the answer to the second question is 'yes' then you might perhaps consider the evening primroses, how they grow, since their classical name, *Oenothera*, comes from two Greek words, *oinos* meaning wine, and *thera*, taste, legend having it that the roots of *Oenothera biennis* are said to encourage a taste for wine.

Whether this is true or not it is certain that the family contains many enchanters, both dwarf and tall, none of whom are difficult, all merely asking for ordinary soil and a place in the sun. All come from the North American continent, though two species, *O. biennis*, the common evening primrose which I suppose everyone knows, and *O. erythrosepala*, having naturalised themselves in this country on sandy and waste places, though never quite in the truly prodigious quantities that you see as soon as you cross the Channel into France.

We tend sometimes to think of the tiresome business of changing plant names as an entirely modern game, but forty years ago Reginald Farrer, the renowned alpine expert, was writing thus: "American botanists have been having such games with the Evening Primroses that there is really no knowing what is what, unless we ignore all those superfluous fal-lals, and stick simply to the good old name without troubling our heads with *Lavauxia, Pachylophus*,

29

Galpisia, Chylisma, Meriolyx, Onagra, Anogra, and all the other tiresome anagrams into which our thicker-blooded-than-water friends across the Atlantic have lately been mangling the Evening Primroses". I should think so too.

Evening Primrose is, by the way, half a misnomer, since a good many of the species and among them some of the most ravishing, open by day and go to bed in the evening, when others of the family are just unfolding. *O. acaulis* is one of these: a very dwarf little thing, no more than six inches high, which bears pure white trumpets by day, the flowers gradually turning to pale pink as they fade away in the evening. This plant, a sweetie, is also known as *O. taraxacifolia.*

Another day-bloomer, but also at night too, and quite my favourite among all the Evening Primroses, is *O. missourienses* (Syno. *macrocarpa*), a truly magnificent plant. Low-growing, with handsome narrow pale green leaves, it bears spear-like buds of green, beautifully spotted with red, which open to great ravishing chalices of pure citron yellow that are an endless joy from July onwards. It comes with the greatest of ease from seed, as indeed do most if not all of the tribe, and probably looks at its best trailing over a big rock or flopping over a dry wall. Queenly, I think, is the word for it: truly queenly.

It is many years since I first grew *O. odorata,* strictly a biennial, though one never need worry about that, since it is always prodigal in seeding itself everywhere. This, as its name implies, is sweetly scented, as indeed are several other species. It is also a true evening bloomer, though there are always a few of its refined, tender creamy-yellow flowers still open as far as mid-morning. It is also capable of a sort of magic trick. Indeed one of the most fascinating sights I ever saw in my garden was to stand one hot summer evening and watch, before my very eyes, the flowers of *O. odorata* unfurling petal by petal, as if excited by some

30

hidden spring, from the slender soft coppery buds. This too flowers for most of the summer. William Robinson, the famous Victorian gardener, incidentally called it the most interesting flower he had ever seen in a garden at night.

O. fruticosa, also known as sundrops, is a worthwhile plant too, perennial, about one foot high, covered with medium-sized deep yellow flowers, again over a long period. It looks well in the front of the border but it is, perhaps, not long-lived, a remark I base on the fact that, after enduring even the scourge of the winter of 1963, it unhappily gave up its ghost in the miserable protracted winter of 1969–70, so that I must now set about acquiring it again.

Similar to *Fruticosa* is *Glauca*, a handsome thing of sub-shrubby growth, again yellow-flowered and long in bloom. An even finer plant is 'Fraseri'. Another good one is *O. speciosa*, with many large white flowers which gradually turn, like those of *O. acaulis,* to delicate rose. It is a true perennial and may be increased with ease from cuttings, division or seed. There is also a true pink variety, *rosea*, which I confess I don't know but which is reputed to be equally good. Nor do I know *O. tetragona* 'Riparia', but that excellent plantsman, Roy Elliott, sings its praises warmly, saying it "is a constant source of delight from July until late September". He confers the same accolade on *O. trilota*, another biennial which obligingly seeds itself everywhere. In heaping further praise on *O. speciosa* he finds it masquerading under as "impressive a range of aliases as there are forms of spaghetti on an Italian menu".

As he says, and as Farrer implied forty years ago, "heigh-ho for the botanist", or a plague on them, whichever you prefer. If you think the botanists as tiresome as I do you'll probably settle for a glass of wine.

[7]

The iris family is so large and so widely distributed across the world that it would require considerable space to deal even cursorily with the species alone, quite apart from the countless hybrids of the bearded iris which come new on to the market every year. The word 'iris', by the way, is from the Greek, meaning a rainbow, though the botanical name for the section of bearded irises is pogon, which sounds more like a prehistoric mammal than a flower.

Not only is the iris family widely distributed (though confined to the northern hemisphere), but it is a flower whose history extends far back in time. It has been well said of it that it "graced the earth when the world was young". For centuries it has made appearances in history, art, literature and medicine. It is not improbable that "the lilies of the field" which we are bidden to consider in the Bible were in fact not lilies at all, but irises. Whether this is so or not, it is beyond dispute that the iris has not only been known and loved for its beauty for at least 2,000 years; it has become a symbol, a resplendent emblem to which all the arts have paid their tribute.

But where does medicine come in? Because centuries ago, it would seem, practically every medicinal virtue was attributed to it. It was said to cure insomnia, ailments of the chest, colic and snake bite, pains of childbirth and ulcers. It was even claimed that it would remove freckles. Today

(i) *Dahlia, Phalaris arundinacea* cta', *Hosta lancifolia, Polygonum amplexicaule, Artemisia* sp. etc.

(ii) *Dahlia* and variegated grass *Phalaris arundinacea* 'Picta'

(i) *Abutilon vitifolium* 'Album'

(ii) *Abutilon × suntense*

its medicinal purposes are confined to a little-known, and I imagine little-used, purgative derived from a poisonous American species, *I. versicolor*. Both the Greeks and Romans used its roots or rhizomes in perfumery and apparently at one period of time a pigment, Iris Green, made from the flowers of *I. florentina*, was much in favour with painters.

Nor are these the end of the family virtues. Not the least of them, to my mind, is a distinction the iris shares with the crocus: namely that of offering us flowers for more than half the year. January has scarcely begun before the little yellow flowers of *I. danfordiae* are in bloom, to be followed by the glorious *I. histrioides,* dwarf too and richly purple, blooming several weeks earlier than the better known *I. reticulata* and its many hybrids, ranging in colour from Cambridge blue to the richest velvety claret. All these, however, are beaten for sheer earliness and length of flowering time by *I. stylosa* (correctly *I. unguicularis*) that regal beauty which starts to throw up its taper-like buds as early as October and goes on and on, with increasing generosity, defying November, December, January, February and March, and emerging still in unbelievable, delicate triumph in April.

There is also a dwarfer sister to this beauty, *I. cretensis,* which has been well compared with the goblets of *Crocus byzantinus*. This I have seen only once (and never at any time in a catalogue) and this was along the Italian Riviera between Nice and San Remo, where an enlightened municipality had planted drifts of it along the roadside, its delicate little blossom as pure as the wintry blue sky above. So many people, however, fail with *I. stylosa* (of which there is a rare clear white form) that perhaps its needs may be set out again.

Since it comes from Algeria the first of these is full sun. There is no better place for it, in fact, than at the foot of a southern house wall. There it should have its feet in the poorest of soils or better still in old mortar rubble, where a process of severe starvation will ensure the long harvest of flowers. Always, then, starvation; and next to starvation, permanence. Once established, it is better that this iris should never be moved. To do so is to deprive it of flowering strength, from which it will take as much as two or three years to recover. By contrast *I. tuberosa* likes it rich. And what a rich extraordinary creature it is; I make no excuse for describing its flowers, as I have done before, as a combination of green and parsonic black, surely one of the most striking the garden can give.

Finally, what of the ever-increasing regiments of the bearded irises, now garlanded in such a range of resplendent uniforms, from palest mauve and primrose to regal oranges, purples, coppers, purest shades of rose and dramatic, burning browns? They are now not merely regiments but legions, making the old purple flag iris of yesterday seem almost a joke. Alas, glorious as they are, you need to be a millionaire to keep up with them, their prices climbing as high as £5 a root, a pretty stiff whack to pay for a plant which, unlike *I. stylosa*, offers only the briefest of glories. Not that one should discount or deride a century or so of hybridisation. Rather one should marvel that the ancient flower has kept its pristine, classical form and for all its new regalities has not yet descended to vulgarity.

One thing, however, is certain. The future will surely hold more and more rainbows to spread their iridescence across our horticultural sky.

[8]

On a warm and very beautiful June afternoon, a friend and I, both of us keen gardeners, decided to shoot ourselves. The arrangement, as in some ludicrously comic opera, was that I shoot him first and then he would shoot me afterwards. Happily this Gilbertian situation **was** never realised and I will now proceed to explain how and why it ever came to be thought up in the first place.

There were two causes, one general, one particular. The general one was that we were visiting a garden called Nymans, in Sussex, owned by the Countess of Rosse and maintained by the National Trust. Very well maintained too, since the garden is very large and only half a dozen gardeners are employed. On that particular afternoon, it was in all its ethereal early summer glory, a great pageant of giant rhododendrons, azaleas, shrub roses, fiery embothriums and many splendid specimens of that loveliest of viburnums, *V. plicatum* 'Mariesii'. It was all enough to make any ordinary gardener weep and the viburnum alone was enough to turn one's thoughts towards self-destruction.

Then suddenly we saw an even more celestial sight and then, as if one wasn't enough, another. These were two immense specimens of the so-called Handkerchief Tree or *Davidia involucrata*, in full and glorious blossom. Now I knew all about *Davidia involucrata*, having read it all up at least thirty years ago, but I had never once seen it in flower and it was these two glorious specimens of it, more like trees filled with pure white birds than handkerchiefs, that brought my friend and me to our moment of despair. *Davidia involucrata* comes from China, where it was first discovered by a French Catholic missionary, Père David – hence its name – in 1869. It was not, however, until 1899 that a serious attempt was made to re-discover it and if possible to bring it into cultivation. To that end the firm of Veitch, of Exeter, issued specific instructions to Ernest Henry Wilson that great plant collector (his contributions to the herbaria of the world number over 16,000 specimens and he introduced into cultivation more than 1,000 species previously unknown) to go to China and seek out the *Davidia* and if possible collect seeds of it.

These were his terms of reference: "The object of the journey is to collect a quantity of seeds of a plant the name of which is known to us. This is the *object* – do not dissipate time, energy or money on anything else. In furtherance of this you will first visit Dr A Henry at Szemao, Yunnan, and obtain from him precise data as to the habitat of this particular plant and information on the flora of Central China in general." (Such are the wonders of ideological progress that you can, seventy years later, no longer go to China to collect plants at all.)

Wilson duly set off for China, where Dr Henry sketched for him on a piece of notepaper a tract of country about the size of the state of New York, where a tree of the *Davidia*, the only one Dr Henry had ever seen, was growing. The place was in high mountains in a thinly populated area south of the Yangtse river. All China was, at that time, owing to the Boxer rebellion, in an explosive state and at Patung the head official, genuinely alarmed for Wilson's safety (some hundreds of people had lately been murdered locally), did his utmost to get Wilson to abandon the enterprise; but Wilson, unperturbed, went on.

Finally he reached the area where Dr Henry had seen the *Davidia*. Did the local inhabitants know where it could be found? Oh yes, most certainly, and Wilson, now in a state of high excitement, was duly escorted to the place. There, to his horror, he found that the *Davidia* had been cut down a year before and a house partly built with its timbers. Poor Wilson didn't sleep much that night.

All this was in April. Then, on May 19th, five days south-westward of Ichang, Wilson's luck changed and he came upon a mighty *Davidia*, 50 feet tall, in full blossom. His excitement was so great that he confessed that "I am convinced that *Davidia involucrata* is the most interesting and most beautiful of all trees which grow in the north temperate regions", and this is how he described it: "The distinctive beauty of the *Davidia* is in the two snow-white connate bracts which subtend the flower proper. These are always unequal in size – the larger usually six inches long by three inches broad, and the smaller three and one half inches by two and one half inches; they range up to eight inches by four inches and five inches by three inches. At first greenish, they become pure white as the flowers mature . . . when stirred by the slightest breeze they resemble huge butterflies or small doves hovering amongst the trees."

In due course, Wilson found several other *Davidias* and from them collected a rich harvest of seeds, which were sent back to England. When he finally got back to England himself he found not a single seed, which rather resembles a walnut, had germinated. Some seeds had been sown in strong heat, some in mild heat; some had been soaked in hot water, some in cold; some had been sown in propagating beds outside – all to no avail. It was not in fact until Wilson examined the seeds sown outside that he at last

37

found signs of germination. The frosts of winter had done their work; it was our old friend stratification performing its miracle once again.

Go therefore to Nymans (or Kew) at the end of June or in July and gaze on this incomparable creature in all her celestial glory. And if she should happen to bring tears to your eyes, as she may well do, you can always console yourself that there will be plenty of handkerchiefs on the branches to dry them with!

[9]

Having just recalled that, on a perfect June day, at the superb garden at Nymans in Sussex, a friend and I threatened to shoot ourselves, I must now record that a year or so later, on an equally beautiful day in May, the two of us came very near to repeating our insane threat, the cause on this occasion being another great and beautiful garden, Leonardslee, also in Sussex and almost next door, as it happens, to Nymans. Happily the second threat came to no more than the first had done and instead we enjoyed another memorable afternoon, with England at the rich peak of all her beauty.

Leonardslee is very large and is wholly the work of one man, Sir Edmund Lodger, grandfather of the present owner, no professional designer having had a hand in it. And since the lay-out was begun as far back as 1887 many of the trees – and it is a garden composed almost entirely of shrubs and trees – are now of gigantic size, one Tulip Tree, *Liriodendron tulipifera*, being no less than 112 feet high, a *Cornus controversa* 48 feet high and a *Magnolia campbellii* 62 feet high. But even these are dwarfed by a giant Redwood of 125 feet.

The soil of Leonardslee being entirely free of lime it isn't surprising that camellias, azaleas and rhododendrons are here in great quantity. The plantings of them are indeed prodigal, so much so that on the deep undulating banks

39

that drop down to a series of small lakes far below the house they rise in almost mountainous piles of pink, scarlet, rose, blue, yellow and white, some of the camellias also producing that enchanting stippled effect in red and white which I myself find to be almost their most attractive feature. One of these camellias is 25 feet high and as much across, which is pretty fair going for a camellia, while another, *Camellia japonica variegata* has a circumference of 66 feet, having been a large tree as far back as 1907. The small lakes on the estate are known as Hammer Ponds, being remains of the iron-ore industry of the past, when hammers and furnaces were driven by water power.

Leonardslee also has its Handkerchief Tree, and a very large one it is, but the sight that brought my friend and me for a second time to the point of self-destruction wasn't the *Davidia* but the great masses of *Pieris*, another lime-hating shrub whose fiery red young growth is almost as brilliant as the bracts of a poinsettia. Second only to the *Pieris* was *Acer* 'Chiso', a maple whose young spring foliage gives the impression, from some distance away, of being a mass of most delicate pink blossom. It is a shrub I first saw growing on Lake Maggiore and I have never forgotten it. But even that was perhaps excelled by the exquisitely chaste beauty of *Cornus controversa*, whose white flowers looked almost like a flock of winging angels against the blue May sky.

It is, however, not only the immense variety of trees and shrubs, or their prodigal massing and size, that make Leonardslee so memorable. A great part of its enchantment lies, to my mind, in its superb natural setting. Surrounding it is the ancient forest of St. Leonard and from the terrace in front of the house, whose walls are covered with that delightful rose, the yellow Banksia, you look down on a deep wooded valley in which not a brick or tile or trace of man can be seen. As far as the eye can see there is nothing but a vast mass of woodland, glorious in May-time

Laburnum × *watereri* 'Vossii'

Erica × *darleyensis* 'Silberschmelze' and white daffodils.

) *Phlox* 'Norah Leigh' and *Onopordum acanthium*

(ii) *Phlox* 'Norah Leigh'

Cornus kousa (2)

with its infinite variations of green as oaks and beech and chestnut and birch and conifers break into leaf, a situation of such magnificence that it must surely be one of the most superb in the whole of Southern England. Indeed if you should happen to come across one of these belly-achers who are always declaring that the English countryside is being wiped out of existence I suggest you grab him by the scruff of his neck and set him down on this terrace and let him drink in not only the sweetness of that lovely old Scotch double yellow wallflower, 'Harpur Crewe', which grows under the walls of the house, but all the sweetness of the world below. It would be a poor heart that didn't then feel prompted to offer up a prayer of thanks for its heritage.

There is, however, one drawback to 'Leonardslee'. Splendid though it is, it suffers from the restriction of being almost wholly a spring garden. In consequence it is open to the public only on selected days (Wednesdays, Thursdays, Saturdays and Sundays) during May. It lies on the main Horsham–Brighton road (A. 281), forty miles from London and eighteen from Brighton. There isn't a signpost saying "This way to Paradise" but I have a strong feeling that there ought to be.

[10]

The discovery of *Davidia involucrata*, the Handkerchief Tree, is not the only botanical excitement to have come out of China in the past fifty years or so. I have long been fascinated by another. I refer to *Viburnum farreri*, one of the most delightful of an attractive family and without doubt one of the most precious of winter-flowering things, with its clusters of white tubular-shaped flowers, tinged pink in bud.

It was in February 1914 that an expedition to China long dreamed of by Reginald Farrer at last got under way, its object being to explore the remote northerly province of the Kansu-Tibet border from North to south. This distant and primitive area was specifically chosen 'in the hope of finding its flora more resistant and useful in the British climate than the softer productions of Yunnan and Szechwan' and also because the 'southern border provinces have been, and are still being worked by English horticultural collectors such as Ward and Forrest, whereas the Kansu March remained a perfectly virgin field'.

'Virgin' hardly describes it. For all the wild beauty of its mountains and valleys, crowded as they were with masses of wild apricot and plum blossom, the place was pretty fearsome, the inns being bug ridden, the landlords uncivil and food hard to come by. Nevertheless, on 16th April of that year a piece of botanical history was made.

For years *Viburnum fragrans* had been one of the best known and best loved of all garden plants all over Northern China. What wasn't known was whether the plant was truly indigenous – native to that place – or if not where its place of origin might be. It was Farrer's hope that somewhere during that remote expedition he would find out.

On 16th April his hopes were realised. For the first time he began to see the viburnum in its wild state, at first only in small and isolated quantities, 'but soon in such quantity and such situations that one could no longer doubt that here this most glorious of flowering shrubs was truly indigenous'.

Not only was this discovery highly satisfying in itself; it was supplemented some time later when Farrer saw the viburnum in full glory at the very feet of the Da Tung Alps, in cottage gardens in 'so high and cold a situation of that cold bleak region that even corn will not ripen there, except perhaps in one season out of three'.

All this rightly induced Farrer to foretell that the viburnum would surely be perfectly hardy in Britain, which it most certainly is. 'May it soon yield us the secular glory of the superb bushes that it makes in the yards of the Prince of Jorni or the great Green Temple at Lanchou – gracious arching masses, ten feet high and more across, whose naked boughs in spring, before the foliage, become one blaze of soft pink spikelets, breathing an intense fragrance of heliotrope.

'The white form, indeed, is pure and long as the best of forced white lilac, but my heart goes out yet more specially perhaps to the enormous commoner pink type, whose blushing stars glisten as if built of crystals, after the pleasant fashion of so many spring flowers, which is shared only, among summer ones, by the gross fleshiness of begonias.

'Nor when the flowers are gone and the delicate foliage

developed, is the work of the viburnum finished. For now appear the glowing glossy scarlet fruits, hanging all over the bush in pendant clusters of jewel work; these you eat with avidity and good result, as long as you remember to throw away the unwholesome kernel.'

I have now been growing *Viburnum fragrans* for forty years but I have never yet seen the pure white variety, nor have I ever been tempted to eat the fruits. What I have done, however, is to note an odd change in the habit of this delightful tree.

When I first grew it its flowering period lasted from about December almost into April. But over the past few years, for some inexplicable reason, it has begun to flower much earlier, often as early as mid-October, its full flush coming in November or December. As a result its flowering season is virtually finished by early January when only a few sparse blossoms remain. I can offer no explanation for this. Nor do I know if other gardeners have had the same experience. It may simply be that the change of habit is peculiar to my own garden.

This is a good moment to mention that there is now an improved variety of *Viburnum farreri*, offered under the name of *Viburnum × bodnantense* 'Dawn'. This not only has much longer flowers than the other type but also has the added virtue of flowering, as this type used to, over a longer period. It is most certainly a worthy addition to an already excellent and highly-rewarding family.

[11]

If you drive southwards out of London on A.20 you will
eventually come to the village of Charing, where the road
forks, the left hand route going to Canterbury, the other
to Hythe and the sea. Charing is a pretty and ancient village
and above it there runs what, in my estimation, is perhaps
the most superb stretch of the North Downs and with it
The Pilgrims' Way. Here the great beechwoods are like
splendid natural cathedrals. In Spring millions of bluebells
make fragrant and glimmering lakes in the less shaded parts
of the woods. In Summer yellow rock-roses shine like fresh-
minted sovereigns on the white chalk. A great variety of
wild flowers abounds and it is sometimes possible even to
see a flower or two of the wild maroon-red columbine.
Farther towards the coast, above Wye, numbers of our
rarest orchids thrive, their habitats jealously and secretly
guarded from would-be predators.

From these high points of downland you can, on fine
clear days, see the sea at Dungeness. Looking in another
direction you can also see the great stretch of man-stitched
landscape stretching away to the South Downs: the huge
quilt of pasture, arable, woodland, orchard, hop-garden,
strawberry field and so on that is both Kent's and England's
splendid heritage.

But across A.20, three or four miles farther south, there
exists a piece of landscape, about 180 acres in extent, that

is not man-made, though man has interfered with it in various ways ever since the Bronze Age. This is Hothfield Common, an infinitely fascinating piece of countryside, in the past a supposed haunt of highwaymen, that is probably the best developed area of acid peat bog and heathland in the county of Kent. This large area, though not strictly Common Land, has survived may vicissitudes, including the second World War.

This survival has been several times threatened: not only during the war by the army, who erected on it numbers of hideous Nissen huts and used it as a tank-training ground but after the war by squatters and gypsies, who moved into the abandoned huts; and then, in the hot summer of 1949, by an extraordinary fire. Fires are, of course, an ever-present risk to forest and open common land, but this fire, which I remember most vividly, was exceptional. Not only did bracken and gorse and heather burn, but the peat itself caught fire and smouldered on and on, for four or five months, underground.

The eventual effect of this prolonged fire on the common's vegetation was very different from what might have been expected. Entirely new plants appeared, in most cases less interesting than those they replaced. Myxamatosis then followed the fire, again with revolutionary effect. Though the southern reaches of the common are fairly thickly wooded with big pines, beeches, hornbeams and Spanish chestnut (the Romans are said to have brought over this tree, the edible nuts of which are reputed to have been part of the staple diet of the soldiery) the more open heath-land parts supported few trees, mostly a few scattered silver birches. The further extension of these birches, which seed very freely, had long been inhibited by rabbits, which were prone to gnaw off the young seedling trees.

But now, with the rabbit population wiped out, the birches were free to grow unhindered and today there are

46

positive forests of them, together with much sallow. Beautiful though they are, these inhibit the growth of other vegetation, notably the more unusual bog plants, by sucking up large quantities of water. This in turn presents a continual problem in conservation, since although the birches have constantly to be thinned out and controlled it is undesirable that they should be totally cleared. Birches provide good cover for a plentiful supply of insect life for such birds as tits and willow warblers.

The common is in fact rich in birds, as it is also in butterflies and vegetation. Fifty four species of birds have been noted, many of them breeding. One hundred and sixteen species of moths and butterflies, including the tiny Orange Underwing Moth, one of our few day-flying moths. Of bog flora there are thirty species and of heathland flora six. Mosses and liverworts provide eighty species.

Another effect of the fire was the appearance, two years afterwards of purple Moor grass, cross-leaved heath and ling and heather. In June, while these are still flowerless and dark of leaf, cotton grass waves among them its pure snow-white pennants, to be followed in August by fields of asphodel, yellow as daffodils among the purples and pinks of heather and ling.

But what really gives Hothfield Common its unique character is that it contains the only remaining valley bogs in Kent. The wet heath and bog habitats in turn support many uncommon plant species and rare mosses. One of the most joyous of these things is the so aptly named Sundew, which looks not at all unlike a delicate golden sea-anemone that has escaped from the shore. This is in fact an insect-eating plant and you can fairly see its tiny anemone-like fingers twitching and itching as it waits to catch and swallow its prey.

Unlike the orchid-rich downland above Wye, the common has only one orchid, the Spotted Orchid, sometimes pale

47

pink, sometimes pure white. But the really water-logged parts of the bog – and even after six weeks of drought in this rare summer of 1970 they were still utterly water-logged – support many species of sphagnum, green, red and yellow-green in colour. Their leaves contain an infinite number of large empty cells which, like a sponge, hold a lot of water. Thus the peat bog carries its own water supply.

The trials and tribulations of war left the common in a wretched state: a dumping ground for old iron, litter and refuse that took some years of hard graft to clear up. Today, thanks to the diligence of both the West Ashford Rural District Council and the Kent Trust for Nature Conservation, the common is in excellent shape. Trails have now been marked out across it and a wooden footbridge built over the bog valley. Seven view points provide an excellent chance to see the common's many variations of vegetation and tree-life and one of them gives a superb view of the rich man-made stitchery of the valley of the young River Stour as it flows out of my own village, Little Chart.

As you look down on this rich fertile pattern you are inevitably struck by the thought that it is not only astonishing, but even miraculous, that the 180 acres of Hothfield Common have managed to survive, in their peculiar wild state, what we fondly call progress: but survive they have. A million vehicles a week must roar past the pines and sweet chestnuts, but the cotton grass waves its snowy plumes in June, the fields of asphodel are yellow in August and the predatory sundew waits with its twitching golden fingers

---

to catch its prey, and one can only hope it will long continue
to do so.

Plates Opposite

(i) *Jasminum polyanthum*
(ii) General view of the house and rockery

49

[12]

Some miles southward of where the sundew grows there is a flat, strange, fascinating piece of sea country, running westwards from Hythe in Kent to the hill on which stands Rye in Sussex and inland to where a ridge above Appledore at last breaks the rich sheep pasture, the great deserted stretches of inland shingle and the criss-crossing of dykes feathered with reeds and illuminated by purple loosestrife and tall mauve-pink marsh-mallows as wild hollyhocks, once inspired someone to the phrase 'five continents and Romney Marsh'.

A unique, separate land, in other words, that makes me think I ought to call this chapter: *The Sea Shore is also a Garden*. Here, inland from the actual shore, kingfishers dart like blue and copper streaks of fire along the dykes, herons poise as if frozen among the reeds and swans sail over on almost savage wings. Here, too, on the famous strong Marsh soil, flower life is rich, the loosestrife and marsh-mallows being particularly splendid, so that it comes as no little surprise to find that the great stretches of dry sand and shingle, which look as if they couldn't support as much as a handful of chickweed, have a correspondingly rich flower life, though vastly different in character, of their own.

When I say vastly different I refer to the fact that the sea-shore has on flowers much the same effect as altitude. The sea-change they suffer rarefies them, reducing them mostly to miniatures, like alpines. How many of these sea-shore flowers the coasts of Britain support I have no real idea, but I judge their name to be legion. There are certainly more than thirty bearing the prefix 'sea', and two with the prefix 'sea-side', these being the sea-side pansy, *V. tricolor curtisii*, with charming yellow flowers, and the sea-side crowsfoot, *Ranunculus baudotii*, which grows in brackish water near the sea.

Among these shore flowers I have several special favourites, of which one, *Geranium Sanguineum lancastrense*, is a little aristocrat good enough for any garden. This loveliest of things, with its flowers of tenderest rose-pink veined with deeper red, doesn't grow on our Southern shores but confines itself to the coast of Lancashire, hence its name. It is hardly ever out of flower from spring to late autumn. It is entirely a no-problem plant, for ever well-behaved and coming true from seed, and no garden should be without it.

Two further favourites of mine and equally lovely, both growing on the Romney Coast, are the magnificent sea-poppy, *Glaucium flavum*, or horned poppy, with its rich near-orange flowers and deep-cut glaucous grey-green leaves. This too is hardly ever out of flower from early summer to October and is always specially lovely in August. (But not for the garden, please. It revels in a starvation diet on shingle.) The second aristocratic beauty is the sea-bindweed (not to be condemned with the hated garden weed) *Calystegia soldanella*, with its huge soft pink trumpets softly veined with white, assuredly one of the loveliest of its tribe.

I have much affection also for two blue beauties, the striking sea-holly, *Eryngium maritimum*, which with its sharp prickly foliage looks as if scissored out of bright blue steel – surely one of our loveliest natives, and Viper's Bugloss *Echium vulgare*, which also loves the starvation of

51

shingle. High in my affection too is the sea-pink, *Armeria maritima*, which of course isn't a pink at all and is probably better known to you as thrift. Great drifts of its little pink hat-pins, looking almost like everlasting flowers, light up the shores all spring and summer long.

The shingle shore is also a vegetable garden. Sea-kale is not so called for nothing. With its plentiful white flowers it is a handsome rather than a pretty plant but it too has an effect of illumination. It is said to have been introduced to Covent Garden from the coasts of Cornwall in 1795. Asparagus is also a maritime plant and consequently, when cultivated, revels in annual dressings of salt. The coasts of Cornwall, Guernsey and Wales also support, appropriately enough, wild leeks. There is also wild carrot and a sea-hogs fennel, both growing near the sea.

I have left till last a plant that doesn't fall into any of the categories I have mentioned. This is sea-buckthorn, an extraordinarily handsome shrub with silvery-green leaves and insignificant greenish flowers which eventually under-go the most wonderful of sea-changes, turning to splendid orange berries which fairly set on fire the sand dunes where, especially in Northern France, it loves to grow.

Yes: the sea shore is also a garden.

[13]

My suspicion that we in England's Green and Pleasant Land are inclined to take greenness and grass for granted is well borne out by a recent experience of two friends of mine. One April they were entertaining two visitors from Argentina. Anxious to show them something of England's 'proud-pied April' they duly motored the visitors about the glorious countryside of mid-Sussex. Never having seen anything like it before the Argentinians were speechless with enchantment until finally one of them exclaimed "But why do you allow the cattle to eat the crops?" The particular crop the cattle were eating was, I need hardly say, grass.

Note that we always speak of grass in the singular, never the plural, no doubt thinking of it merely as that green stuff that has to be shorn down to below an inch on summer Saturday afternoons, thus ignoring the fact that we have a whole legion of native grasses, many of them of enchanting grace and beauty, from the dainty totter-grass of meadows to the lordly tall-as-corn ones that adorn dykes and roadsides. All flesh is grass, the Bible says; and conversely we might say that all grass, eventually, becomes flesh.

In the garden, however, we simply think of all grass as weeds. Even so I have a suspicion that more and more gardeners, possibly having their elbows jogged by the new race of flower-arrangers, are becoming increasingly

53

interested in grasses ornamental. There are a lot of these and most of them are foolproof, some of them so foolproof that they can, if unchecked, become a confounded nuisance. I have clumps of one of these in my borders, always invoking rapturous admiration for its three-foot pink-and-gold variegations, so that I am always glad to give whole sheaves of it away. In spite of this we have to make, from time to time, positively furious onslaughts on it in order to preserve its bed-fellows from total strangulation.

The classical names of most of these grasses will, I fancy, have little or no meaning for the average gardener, who is very unlikely to have heard of *Rhynchelytium repers*, *Tricholaena rosea*, *Hordeum jubatum*, *Panicum violaceum* or upwards of fifty others obtainable commercially. I mention these three for the good reason that they are especially attractive. *Panicum violaceum* has wide flag-like leaves, reminding one of the better-known variegated maize, itself a good and useful plant, and big tassel-heads of green and violet which recall those emblems of office which African chiefs take around with them. *Tricholaena rosea* has silky spikes of wine-rose that turn a dark maroon as they age. *Hordeum jubatum* is feathery, silver-grey and very graceful. All these provide a lot of charm from about July to the late autumn. Another favourite grass of mine is *Festuca glauca*, which is barely six inches high and therefore admirably suited to the rock garden. Its thin, misty blue-grey spikes, making a sort of pin-cushion, are an absolute delight.

This same misty to blue-grey effect is common to many of these ornamental grasses. *Agrostis nebulosa* bears a name that speaks for itself and has much the same cloud effect as gypsophila. *Lagurus ovatus*, about a foot in height, has lovely fur-like heads. *Coix lacryma-jobi* doesn't need to spell out any further that it is Job's Tears, the tears being pea-like seeds, again of a soft pearly grey. *Pennisetum villosum* is a half-hardy annual with a singularly twisted appearance, together with a soft plume of white or sometimes purple. The noblest grass of all and the best known, of course, is *Cortaderia selloana (argentea)*, the Pampas Grass, which I always think needs a special and isolated situation to show off its striking beauty. Its common name comes, of course, from the fact that in its wild magnificence it graces the vast South American *pampas*, though I often think there's good enough reason to call it the Ostrich Feather grass.

Which brings me to another charming aspect of these grasses: their common names. How is this for a necklace of jewels? – Cloud Grass, Animated Oats, Little Quaking Grass, Love Grass, Squirrel Tail Grass, Hare's Tail, Feather Grass, Yellow Bristle Grass, Golden Grass. Many of these are either hardy or half-hardy annuals, though a good number are hardy perennials. Another nice thing about them is that nearly all of them may be dried for winter decoration, when they turn, like the wheat and barley and oats many of them resemble, to soft autumnal shades of gold and in doing so become the delight of flower arrangers. Probably some of them will also perform that same magical trick I used to do as a child with one of our native grasses. You gather the barley-like head and let it rest on your wrist and in no time at all, of its own volition, it creeps, like a bristly mouse, up your arm.

[14]

I have a very warm corner in my gardening heart for the primula family. Not that I know it all that well, for the simple reason that it so so vast, so widely distributed all over the world, that you would have to exchange your mind for an encyclopedia in order to deal with even a part of it. But what can be safely said is that few families attract so much affection, from our beloved primrose, cowslip and oxlip to the richer, taller beauties of Tibet and China and the Himalayas, and offhand I can't name a bad or remotely ignoble plant among them.

Where to begin? That's a problem. The merest glance at Farrer's celebrated book *The English Rock Garden* will show why. Farrer lists no less than 95 pages of primulas, alpine, bog, herbaceous or of garden origin, embracing species from almost every corner of the world. There are in fact over 500 species of primula, enough to satisfy or daunt even the experts. I use the word daunt advisedly, remembering Farrer's often-quoted remark that "a cold awe sweeps across the gardener as he comes at last into the shadow of this grim and glorious name, which, there is no question, strikes terror no less than rapture into the mind of the boldest".

Farrer goes on to tell us that the primula has acquired, and quite unjustly, 'a bad reputation in the garden' – solely, in his view, because generations of gardeners have got into their heads, and obstinately refused to get it out again, the wrong notion that primulas as a whole need damp, dank, shady conditions, a misconception arising possibly from the fact that our own primrose loves the damp and shade of woods and dykes. For many primulas, coming as they do from alpine regions, precisely the opposite is true. "They are," says Farrer, "*children of the broad sunlight* on the high rolling turf of the mountain tops, and the rocks of crest and summit."

At the same time there are of course many primulas that love to have their feet in damp or moist earth or near water. Among these are the candelabra section, which embraces *P. beesiana*, *P. bulleyana*, *P. pulverulenta*, *P. florindae*, and *P. nutans*. The name *pulverulenta* means 'powdered with meal', which is a common characteristic of so many primulas, including *P. auricula*, that lovely alpine with its intense silvery farina on the leaves and glorious bright yellow flowers which has been the parent of so many hybrids in all manner of colours ranging through cream, yellow, mauve, purple, green, white, brown and sherry-gold. I have nothing but adoration for these auriculas, so popular a century or less ago but later, for some inexplicable reason, out of favour. They are easily raised from seed, are exceedingly tough and will endure for years. Also, thank heaven, birds show none of that mischievous interest in them that they reserve for primroses and polyanthus.

Two of the tallest and best of the candelabra group are undoubtedly *P. florindae*, a rich, strong, sweetly scented beauty from Tibet, and *P. pulverulenta*, of which the Bartley strain contains many delicate and delicious shades of pink and rose. Many of these candelabra primulas seed themselves with the utmost freedom, so much so that they may well become an embarrassment if not in fact something of a nuisance. My favourite however is *P. bulleyana* with rich shades of orange, gold and apricot. It is also, in my experience, the longest lasting of this excellent group.

Two other sections offer much delight. The progeny of *P. juliae* now come in many, many shades: sulphur-yellow, lilac, claret, flame, maroon and white, all having the characteristic primrose-shaped flower and many having distinctly coloured leaves. The other section is our dear old friend *P. denticulata* from the Himalayas, often called the drumstick Primula, a name I don't like, even though it describes the flower well. This, one of the earliest primulas to flower, coming as it does in March, is readily raised from seed, but the seedlings may be very variable, ranging from deep rich purple to rather washy mauves, so that a process of weeding out may be necessary in order to secure the more desirable forms. There is also a white variety *P. denticulata* 'Alba', which has its own cool white-green enchantment and comes quite true from seed.

[15]

Fritillary – from the Latin, *fritillus*, a dice-box, hence by
analogy implying a chequer-board, referring us in turn to
the chequered pattern of the flowers of several species,
notably our own snakeshead fritillary, with its lovely
purple bells, *Fritillaria meleagris*, speckled like a guinea
fowl as well as a snake, its native habitat being zealously
guarded in several parts of England. There is also a chaste
white form of this, quite unchequered. Both, greatly
desirable, will naturalize easily.

Fritillary also gives us the names of several butterflies,
the loveliest of which, surely, is *The Queen of Spain Fritillary*, the syllables floating from the tongue like veritable
airy wings themselves. Here again the chequered effect is
implied.

I am writing these words in April when, although the
garden is rich with daffodils, tulips, hellebores, anemones
and a score of other spring glories, there is absolutely no
doubt that the most majestic, most talked-of thing in it is
Fritillaria imperialis, a truly noble creature with its stems of
nearly four feet and its imperial crown of hanging bells in
shades either of orange-red or pure clean yellow. You don't
need to look twice at this striking thing to know that it
belongs to the lily family. Its one disadvantage is that it has
a slightly repugnant odour, though not to my senses as
strong as, for example, *Cytisus × praecox*. The answer to

59

both these things is to plant them well away from the house, preferably against a dark background, so that they may be worshipped from afar. The Crown Imperial comes from fairly large bulbs, which should be planted in the autumn. Though not exactly cheap, I rate them as marvellous value.

Now I don't claim to have grown, or to be familiar with, all the species I am about to mention; I only know that all of them are on the market and a diligent search through catalogues specially devoted to less common bulbs will seek them out. Of *Fritillaria meleagris*, already mentioned, there are four or five variations, 'Artemis' having grey-purple checks, 'Pomona' having violet checks on a white ground, and 'Saturnus', a large-flowered variety, with bright red-violet flowers.

Several of these species come from North America, though a larger number originate in Eastern Europe and Asia Minor, indicating that some of them, like certain tulip species, need a good summer baking to prove successful. It is also only fair to say here that the old oracle Reginald Farrer claimed that the fritillary family had on the whole rather a bad character or, as he put it in his own particular way, were of rather "miffy temper". Now my own way with plants of miffy temper is very simple – out! I have neither time nor patience to stand in prayer over sulkies, however rare, who refuse to spread their sweetness on the air. If they don't love me then I don't love them and swift divorce is the only answer.

Farrer was also decidedly cynical about certain fritillaries having "bells of dingy chocolate and greenish tones, which often appear transfigured by the enthusiasm of those who desire to get rid of them as rich purple' or 'amaranthine violet'." I take this to be a wise injunction to inspect the living flower before you buy or in other words "put not your trust in catalogues", the compilers of which all too

60

often don't know the difference between scarlet and magenta.

However, here are a few more species to seek out. *F. pyranaica* comes, as its name implies, from the Pyrenees. *F. acmopetala* has petals pale green inside, tipped with purple. *F. pallidiflora* comes from Siberia and has, according to one catalogue, yellow tulip-shaped flowers but, according to Farrer, beautiful solid white bells – take your choice. Farrer accords it "a good sound perennial temper". Another authority, Roy Elliott, reminding us that this particular fritillary comes from a level of eight to nine thousand feet, says that in his experience "the bulbs are very apt to rot". His greatest success, apparently, has been with *F. camtschatcensis*, which ranges from Alaska to Japan and has fairly large purple-black flowers. If you get tired of eating potatoes you can, apparently, try bulbs of this fritillary instead. They were so used by Captain Cook and are still eaten, it would seem, by Eskimos. Whether they make good crisps or chips I wouldn't know.

Finally another word or two about the noble Crown Imperial. It has two further virtues that make it so worth while. While many spring flowers, especially shrubs, flower all too briefly, it has a flowering period of a good month or more, in the middle of which it seems to grow in stature and beauty every day. Also, since its bells are pendant it is able to throw off even the heaviest April rain and with me has emerged quite unscathed from a week of extreme nastiness composed of gales, torrential rains and a touch of snow. You can't ask much more of a plant than that.

[16]

It is contended that if we were entirely to evacuate the English landscape, so much of which is man-made, it would return to natural forest within twenty-five years. All this would of course be achieved by seeds, entirely without the aid of man.

The thought inspires me to say that if I were a young man and starting a garden all over again I should have no hesitation in growing not only a great many plants from seed but also a considerable number of trees and shrubs. There are several reasons for this. First, of course, cost: the formidable expense of nursery stock, more especially trees and shrubs, is becoming positively frightening, even if one saves carriage costs, which Heaven knows are frightening enough in themselves, by collecting things from plant centres; second, raising a shrub or tree from seed is a great challenge and great fun, leading to an immense sense of satisfaction as the species mature; third, the task is by no means a difficult one and it is also surprising how soon very many trees and shrubs reach maturity, whether they are grown for blossom or not.

I am fortified in this resolve by the fact that I hardly ever tour my garden without spotting some new self-sown seedling of a tree or shrub, of which the varieties are considerable: cotoneasters, brooms, hollies, conifers, clematis, even roses. Some of these, which appeared only two or three years ago, are now maturing into sizable specimens. One, a seedling *Cupressus*, is eight feet high; other varieties of *Cupressus*, originally raised from seed gathered by a friend in Yugoslavia, have now reached an even greater height, closely followed by a *Cupressus macrocarpa* which, only a couple of summers ago, was no bigger than a child's paint brush. Even this rate of growth is exceeded by the cotoneasters, which are, if anything, rather too rampant.

Naturally one doesn't want a surfeit of commoner things. Where, then, does one get seed of choicer subjects? The answer is that excellent seed-house, Thompson & Morgan, of Ipswich, whose fat seed catalogue listing some 5,000 items I have used for nearly fifty years. Here there are no fewer than 12 pages of shrub and tree seed, many of them uncommon, some rare. There are no fewer than 15 species of maple, the same of berberis, 26 of cotoneaster, 14 of cupressus, 22 of eucalyptus, 16 of magnolia and no less than 46 of rhododendron, many of them rare, ranging in size from $1\frac{1}{2}$ feet to 30 feet. Add to these a couple of dozen hybrids and species of rose, a dozen of erica, a dozen and a half of brooms and another dozen and a half of pines and you begin to get some idea of the vast choice open to the gardener of adventure and patience.

Naturally you can't get everything. There are, for instance, no eucryphias, one of which, *E. glutinosa*, I have extolled as perhaps the choicest shrub of the year. Nor can I find a shrub which is perhaps even more exquisite: the ravishing *Michelia doltsopa*, which is related to the magnolias. This heavenly beauty, which comes from Japan, bears in spring huge floppy blossoms of purest white which give off the most celestial perfume. I must confess I have never seen it growing in this country, though I believe it does do so, but only in Madeira, where its glorious January–February display takes the breath away.

Nevertheless there are many things almost as choice.

63

Seed is available, for instance, of *Davidia involucrata*, the Handkerchief Tree, *Vitis coignetiae*, the huge-leaved vine whose praises I have so often sung, is also here. *Fremontia californica* and *Carpenteria californica*, the one with generous yellow poppy-like flowers, the other with white, are available; so, to my surprise, is *Hibiscus mutabilis*, whose flowers that change from pale pink to deep red as the day goes on, I have described. A relative of the citrus family *Poncirus trifoliata*, a shrub with stout pines and bearing miniature yellow oranges, is available. This shrub, though its little oranges are not much good to eat, makes a dense and forbidding hedge. So too does *Eleagnus angustifolia*, a great favourite of mine with its shiny silver leaves, delicate silver-yellow flowers and golden-orange fruits much loved by blackbirds. My specimen gets madly raided every week or two by flower arrangers, and deservedly so.

As to other fruits, I note both persimmon and pomegranate, the latter of which, with its reddish-orange fuchsia-like flowers, I find enchanting. It is perfectly easy from seed and will make an endearing pot-plant. Another silver-leaved shrub also bearing scarlet fruits in the autumn and related to the *Eleagnus* tribe is *Shepherdia argentea*, sometimes called the Buffalo Berry. Still another orange-fruiting shrub, this time from China, is *Stranvaesia davidiana*, and still another, *Sarcococca ruscifolia*. The charming pittosporums, also much-loved by flower arrangers, sit side by side with four varieties of *Pieris*, all peat-lovers, one with fiery red almost poinsettia-like leaves when young, all with lily-of-the-valley-like flowers.

Scope for adventure indeed. And if you are a *bonsai* fan there is also plenty of scope for skill. As to culture, don't forget our old friend 'stratification'. This simply means sowing the seed outside in winter, leaving it exposed to hard frosts in order to break dormancy. This is also the way to germinate peach and apricot stones. My two sons,

Fritillaria imperialis

when boys, grew scores of peach-trees from stones, eventually fruiting them quite successfully. Finally, if you like maple-syrup, *Acer saccharum* will give you just that, with a glorious bonus of orange and crimson autumn foliage thrown in.

Plates Opposite
(i) *Senecio cineraria* forms
Large 'White Diamond' – Small 'Silver Dust'
(ii) *Pyrus salicifolia* 'Pendula', *Veronica virginica, Onopordum acanthium, Artemisia* sp., *Gypsophila* sp., White Mallow

[17]

This chapter is not directed to gardeners who like dahlias a foot across, chrysanthemums as big as footballs or vegetable marrows as fat as elephants' behinds. Nor, I suspect, will it appeal much to those who seek to grow vast spikes of perfectly opened gladioli or sweet peas with seven or eight flowers on a stem. It is entirely about little things, that is to say not necessarily absolute midgets or miniatures but simply small enchanters which for all their smallness will give a lot of reward.

First the epimediums. A friend of mine calls them 'appy mediums and the description is by no means inapt. Happy they certainly are. For some reason you don't see them very often and I can't think why; nor is there much written of them in gardening books, which seems to me an unfair slight on these fairy-like creatures which begin to expend their beauty as early as March and are utterly unexacting in their cultural demands. They throw up a dense mass of handsome oval-shaped leaves delightfully veined in yellow-green and copper which turn dry and brown by winter's end, when they must be shorn off so that the delicate trembling spikes of flower are free to open. The commonest colour in these flowers is a pale but by no means washy yellow and there is also a tangerine variety and one that is between pink and red. Not the least of this plant's virtues is that it is also a good ground cover.

Wallflowers are so well known that you might well think there was nothing new to be said about them. But the cheiranthus family offers several fascinating treasures that are all too little known. The sweetest of these – and by sweet I really mean sweet, since its scent is of the most exquisite richness – is probably also the oldest. Now known as 'Harpur Crewe' after a clergyman of that name who nursed it along in the 19th century, it was known and loved long, long before that and deservedly so. Its short spikes of brilliant yellow are fully double, utterly adorable and come in April and May. There is also a paler variety called 'Moonlight'. Another fascinating and unusual wallflower is *Cheiranthus mutabilis* (now *C. sempervirens*) which, as its name implies, changes colour as it grows, beginning a pale yellow, then turning to a browny-orange and finally to a soft parma violet. But remember that none of these wall-flowers are long-lived. They are, however, easily raised from cuttings and you can now also get seed of 'Harpur Crewe'.

Flowering at the same time as these wallflowers is another elegant little treasure all too rarely seen: *Prunus tenella nana*. This is a dwarf almond, hardly two feet high, whose branches are thickly covered, provided birds leave them alone, with true pink almond blossom. But take care – this little beauty is also highly possessive. It suckers so badly in fact that it must be kept in check with a ruthless hand. It should be pruned hard after flowering in order to induce new growth for the following year.

Another family of much enchantment and highly suitable for a small garden are the dwarf sallows. Coming a little earlier than the almond they have the characteristic silver pussy catkins which later turn, as with the larger sallows, a pure fluffy gold, providing feasts for bees. There are several of these dwarfs and the best way of choosing them, I fancy, is not from catalogues but at a garden centre.

Two other little treasures recently came my way and I had seen neither of them before. One is a variegated strawberry, its variegations being in exactly the same tones as those of a little hypericum I like very much, namely bright green, bright pink and gold. This is completely prostrate and has a good companion in a variegated version of our old friend London Pride, which is green and gold with reddish flowers. Both sit happily on a dry wall with another pleasant little dwarf for company, the silver-grey *Oxalis adenophylla*, with its curiously twisted leaves and soft pink flowers. This looks altogether too delicate to have come from the harsh air of the Falkland Islands, but at least that fact ensures that it is quite hardy, however delicate it may look.

I have never been particularly fond of the familiar snowberry-tree bearing the awful name of *Symphoricarpos racemosus* (*S. albus*). It has always seemed to me to be one of those cinderella plants to be relegated to the back of dingy shrubberies and there to pine away a rather dim existence. But it is well worth noting that there is a variegated version of this, with yellow and green leaves, far less coarse than the type, never more than 3–4 feet high, and bearing no berries, which is a wholly admirable little shrub for small gardens, leafless all winter but quite luminously charming all summer long.

Finally I make no apology for mentioning yet again one of the most splendid, the most enchanting dwarfs – the prostrate evening primrose *Oenothera missourienses*, surely one of the loveliest things ever to be introduced into our gardens. From the moment in April when its first bright crimson shoots appear to the last flourish of its wide candid yellow flowers in November it repeats its riches for us over and over again. I love it not only for the sheer freshness of its yellow saucers open fully before breakfast on warm summer mornings but also for the promise of next day riches contained in its long pointed buds splendidly spotted with scarlet. A treasure indeed – quite hardy, quite perennial and easily raised from seed.

[18]

For some years now I have excluded all bedding geraniums from my scheme of things. It isn't that I completely dislike such varieties as 'Paul Crampel', 'Lady Ilchester', 'Queen of Denmark', 'Gustav Emich', 'Winston Churchill' and a host of similar varieties. It is simply that when faced with the worst an English summer can offer they just give no reward. There is no more dismal sight in the gardening calendar than a bed of scarlet geraniums drooping, rotten with grief, under prolonged and heavy August rain. Always they cry for sun and more sun, heat and more heat. When these fail to bestow their blessings you might just as well grow cabbages.

All this is not to say that I use no geraniums at all in my summer schemes. I do indeed use them but at the same time confine myself only to varieties with variegated leaves. With these you have a double bet. If the summer should be good you can be sure of having flowers; if it turns sour you have the compensation of leaves, some of them very beautiful, all of them fascinating. In fact with these variations, of which there are considerable numbers, you are finally insured.

The range of these markings and variegations is pretty wide, starting with the golden and silver tricolors on the one hand and going on to the black-leaved varieties such as 'Mephistopheles' and 'Black Vesuvius' on the other.

These black-leaved varieties are mostly miniatures, not growing more than eight inches or so high, and are therefore not as suitable for growing outdoors, in my opinion, as some taller and larger leaved varieties. This is not to deny them singular beauty, with their satanic scarlets glowing fiercely against the black leaves, but it is simply unfair to them to let them get lost in the herd. They are better on the greenhouse bench, though I feel sure they would look rewarding in a stone sink or even on the top of a dry wall.

I think my favourites among these variegations are the butterfly-leaved varieties. These have a butterfly mark of distinct contrasting tone in the centre of the leaf, the outer edges of which can be in delicious lime or apple green. There are not a great many of these butterflies, but some of the best known are 'Happy Thought', 'Crystal Palace Gem', 'Freak of Nature' and 'Black Cox'. Very often a plant will produce not one or two variations in its leaf markings but several more. In other cases the butterfly is too indistinct. In a variety called 'The Boar' (what a name to give to a flower) it is a darkish maroon-brown, with the petal edges bright apple green.

Though the tricolors, both silver and gold, are so called they are more often than not quadricolors, holding infinite variations of gold, red, green and purple-brown. It is not uncommon to find among them a plant of which no two leaves are alike. In the silver-leaved and silver tricolors 'Lass O' Gowrie' and 'Miss Burdett Coutts' are two remarkable survivors, often confused, dating from well over a hundred years ago. Not quite so old but certainly dating from Victorian times and certainly as well loved are 'Caroline Schmidt', 'Mrs Parker', 'Chelsea Gem' and 'Flower of Spring'. These, I find, go particularly well with dense beds of *Verbena rigida* (*V. venosa*) which, even in the wettest of summers, never surrenders and always holds its stiff purple flowers gloriously.

71

Here I must put in an enthusiastic word for a geranium which, though not belonging to the tricolors and variegations, is nevertheless an admirable plant which should, I feel, be in any garden. You see this ivy-leaved variety all over France and Switzerland, raining its bright pink trusses of flowers from balconies, urns, pots and window boxes, a most prolific and loveable thing. 'Ville de Paris' is so easily propagated that in three years I have worked up a stock of several hundreds from the half dozen original sprigs I first brought back from France. To the pale pink variety there has now been added a darker one and equally good it is.

Lastly a variegated ivy which is entirely new to me but quite enchanting – 'Sussex Lace', which admirably describes its delicious green-and-gold lace-work. You may be sure I shall have my propagating needles working hard at this one.

[19]

I have a certain passion for white flowers. At the same time I am fully aware that great numbers of people take an entirely opposite view and cannot tolerate the thought or sight of white flowers at any price. I recall a rather select luncheon party a couple of summers ago. As we sat down to table it suddenly seemed to me that my hostess had become singularly tense. This state of affairs grew rapidly worse until she at last sprang to her feet, seized a vase of flowers from the centre of the table and threw it out of the window.

"I can't bear them! I can't bear them! I simply can't bear them!"

The offending objects were a couple of white arum lilies. Useless for me to point out the classical purity of the flower, its likeness to a horn or certain types of sea-shell or that its elegance was most striking when it grew wild.

"Horrible. Can't bear them. Remind me of funerals."

I had, needless to say, heard it all before and now, as always, failed to understand why white should have this illogical, melancholy association. But there it was. Illogical or not, it had deeply permeated the heart and consciousness of my hostess and would for ever remain.

As for myself I can only say that I grow more and more fond of white flowers as I grow older. Lovely as they are in their many individual forms I love them for their power to light up the garden. I am writing these words on an abysmally humid, dark, rain-soaked morning in July. The colours of flowers are washed out or wreathed in wet mist. The only ones not to suffer from these afflictions are those of pure white. They shine through the gloom of rain with a remarkable candescence, like lamps.

Where to begin with white? Lilies would seem to be the obvious starting point – not only arums but also those noble and so aptly named Madonnas, so pure as to be almost saintly. But I also have a certain crackpot affection for white in roses. What lovelier thing than that old Hybrid Perpetual, 'Frau Karl Druschki'? or the ravishing 'Madame Alfred Carrière'? or that most lovable and prolific of ramblers 'Félicité et Perpétue'? or the still older white *centifolia* with its flowers all crimped so as to give the effect of shells? Nor are there many better white roses in cultivation than the present-day 'Iceberg', so strong and prolific, its flowers having a merest flush of cream deep in the heart. Nobody is going to persuade me that any of these beauties inspire the slightest melancholy.

I go strongly too for white pinks and also white campanulas, both tall and dwarf. I also have considerable affection for a very old white lilac which came originally from my great-grandmother's garden. She was, when I was a small boy, well into her eighties and my impression is that the lilac was even older. Age hasn't diminished the power of my own tree to give prodigious masses of pure white flower every spring.

No sooner has the ancient lilac given its tower of purest white than the philadelphus follow with theirs: such ethereal grace, such fragrance. Spanning the two of them comes my favourite magnolia, *M. denudata*, unblemished white, a tree of perfect chalice-shaped lamps, infinitely to be preferred, in my view, to *M.* × *soulangiana*, the one more often seen. When all these have gone come the eucryphias, all white again, of which *E. glutinosa* is the latest and best.

White phloxes and white dahlias light up August and September, by which time the dear old 'Frau Karl Druschki' will have begun her generous act of giving a second flowering.

And then the winter-spring whites: white crocus, Christmas roses, snowdrops, white violets, white hyacinths and, perhaps most elegant of all, the white lily-flowered tulips with their reflexed petals of serenest grace. These are utter perfection and she would be a brave woman indeed who could throw those out of the window in my presence.

Little acts of transformation sometimes occur to give white where white never was. The old pink-purple honesty will sometimes throw up white progeny, a mystery which has also happened in my garden with another old favourite, the silver-leaved pink lychnis. This accidental treasure looks, from a distance, to be pure white, but closer inspection will show a wonderfully delicate stitchery of pink in the heart of the flower.

Many families of flowers either have no white or only whites of dubious kind. The white *Geranium dalmaticum* might be cut out of old newspaper and I have yet to see a really good white penstemon and I await the day when someone will give us a really pure white day lily to join the many aristocrats that now adorn that happy family.

[20]

The behaviour of birds (both kinds) may be likened, I sometimes think, to the peace of God: it passeth all understanding. For centuries men have been making the mistake of trying to understand women, not appreciating that women neither need nor want to be understood: merely to be loved. In much the same way we gardeners are now trying to understand birds, their apparently fickle nature and what makes them mischievously ravage so many of the plants we love.

I am prompted to these observations by a recent article by Mr Roy Hay, who had received and dealt with an extensive pile of correspondence on the subject of why birds attack certain flowers not only without apparent reason but also apparently out of heartless ingratitude for the food that gardeners put out for them in winter. The greater part of Mr Hay's correspondents were firm in the conclusion that the more food you put out for birds the more they will attack your plants, and with this view, very reluctantly Mr Hay agreed.

For my part I do not agree. It is my firm conviction, based on something like forty years of gardening, that the behaviour of birds in gardens is wholly illogical – that is from the human point of view. It is also my experience that the apparently mischievous and fickle behaviour of birds towards certain flowers tends to go in cycles. Whether you feed birds or not there is no atom of consistency in what they will do to your plants as soon as your back is turned.

There can be few gardeners who have not suffered painful and infuriating experiences of this kind. I give now a few of my own. For many years my forsythia, ignored by birds, was a ravishing sight. Suddenly birds decided this wouldn't do at all and began to ravage it unmercifully, so that for ten years not a single bud was allowed to blossom. Now, with equal and inexplicable suddenness, they ignore it again, so that once more it blossoms splendidly. So with polyanthus: unmolested for years, they were suddenly mercilessly attacked. The cure, wholly successful for several seasons, was black cotton. Then, last year, even that failed to deter. In desperation I resorted to ginger. It worked. This year black cotton is again the successful protector.

I had for many years a bush of that most bewitching of viburnums, the richly scented *V. carlesii*, and another of *V. × burkwoodii*. Suddenly, for a period of five years, every bud on the two bushes dropped before opening. The cause, I was told by a horticulturalist far more experienced than I, was unknown. Moreover the disease, as disease it evidently was, was spreading everywhere, even to Wisley. I despaired. Then one day I appealed – Wisley having given little comfort in its advice – to another expert. His answer was simple: birds. Again it was black cotton to the rescue and now the viburnums again bloom happily, drenching the spring air with that incomparable fragrance of theirs. Precisely the same thing happened with my wisterias and again the same cure worked.

Aubrieta, over many years, flourished unmolested. Now birds have decided that it makes delightful nesting material and heartlessly pull it to pieces. Last year a pair of missel thrushes, which as a boy I called screaming thrushes, decided that the silver foliage of *Centaurea gymnocarpa*

77

would serve the same purpose. They moved into attack on a May morning. I replied with a pair of barn cloches, thinking that the flash of glass in the sun would be adequate scare. Not so; I had neglected to close the cloche ends and the thrushes seemed to find it even greater fun to hop into the little glass house and fetch out the silver wallpaper for their new home. The cloche ends having eventually been put on, the birds, infinitely puzzled, came back almost to sneer through the glass, as if much chagrined by the mean behaviour of the wretched fellow who had put it there.

There were springs when crocuses were tugged to pieces. It never happens now. The birds apparently like young lettuces better. But sometimes forget-me-nots also make tempting nesting material, though I confess that it is not an unpretty sight to see a goldfinch flicking delicately through the air with a bright blue sprig of flower in its beak.

Constantly we ask ourselves *why* do they do it? I also constantly ask myself another question: why, suddenly, and for no apparent reason, do birds of one kind or another desert a garden? I am thinking of chaffinches – 'pinks' I used to call them as a boy. I read somewhere, only the other day, that the chaffinch is Britain's commonest bird. So it used to be in my garden, some pairs being so tame that they would come and eat cake out of your hand on a summer afternoon. Now, with us, the chaffinch has become a rare bird, so that I get into a state of positive excitement when I see one shyly picking up breakfast crumbs among the hordes of starlings, sparrows, tits, robins, blackbirds and thrushes that busily congregate by the kitchen door. Why, oh! why has the chaffinch thus deserted us?

Yet who am I to complain? In the wretched, protracted winter of 1969–70 I suppose we put out more food for birds than ever before. Result? Contrary to the theories of Mr Hay and his correspondents the birds responded by behaving impeccably. Not a bud of forsythia, wisteria or viburnum was touched, not a head of polyanthus, not one goblet of crocus.

It doesn't make sense? of course it doesn't make sense. Birds, of whatever sort, aren't supposed to make sense. For that reason we say that we don't understand them; but my own theory is that we should simply say to them (both kinds of course) "for all thy faults we love thee still".

[21]

I often think that that much-maligned institution, the British climate, deserves a better reputation. I thought of it more especially on Christmas Day, 1972, when a year reported to be the driest for fifty years lay behind us. The day dawned from behind a lovely unfurling curtain of light cloud, purest pink against an already rich blue sky. As this pink faded, leaving the clouds to disperse, the morning became all brilliant unblemished gold and the air like spring.

Over the lawn trembling clouds of gnats danced as they might have done on an evening in June. Robins were singing in an atmosphere that had in it neither malice nor any other sound. The illusion that it was already spring took me into the garden in order to discover for myself if it was fantasy or reality.

Reality it was. By the house wall the branches of *Hamamelis mollis* were all alight with twisted stars of brightest yellow. This exquisite thing never fails to show its first flowers on or about the shortest day and now it was

---

Plates Opposite

(i) *Cheiranthus* 'Harpur Crewe'
(ii) *Tradescantia virginiana*
(iii) *Auricula*
(iv) *Geranium sanguineum* 'Album'

(ii)

(iv)

(i)

(iii)

(v)

more than half way to its fullest beauty. There sometimes comes a moment when blue-tits decide to gather on it, turning the whole thing into a delicious and delicate Chinese painting.

It wasn't the only shrub coming to full bloom. *Prunus subhirtella* had already been blooming for a week or two, its pale pink blossoms exquisite as a Chinese painting too. This tree has the admirable virtue of being able to go back to sleep if the weather turns really cold and then of waking up, in renewed glory, when it turns mild again. Close by it were more yellow stars, those of our old friend the winter jasmine, *Jasminum nudiflorum*, a positive galaxy of them, – strange to think that when it was first introduced it wasn't considered to be hardy and was thought to need the protection of a glass-house.

This was actually growing up the house wall and all underneath it was a thirty-foot row of *Iris stylosa*, its many flowers like delicate mauve orchids – surely the loveliest of all the things that our maligned climate offers us from November to April. Almost as exquisite were a few heads of nerines, a pure white one, still blooming as bravely as if it were summer. Close by them were two other unfailing beauties, *Crocus laevigatus* and the first of the winter aconites. The little stars of the crocus, almost the same colour as the irises, had already been coaxed wide open by the touch of sun – the first of many hundreds of winter crocus that will span the five months from December to April.

These were only the beginning of the winter joys. I still

Plates Opposite

(i) *Dianthus*   (ii) *Fuchsia* 'Thalia'
(iii) *Daphne* x *Burkwoodii*   (iv) Variegated Pelargoniums
(v) *Convolvulus tricolor*   (vi) *Oenothera odorata*

hadn't come to *Mahonia bealei*, with its handsome holly-like foliage and its long racemes of yellow flower, not at all unlike lily-of-the-valley to look at and almost exactly like lily-of-the-valley in perfume. It was slightly ahead of two other delightful things, a pink *cydonia japonica* (*Chaenomeles*), its buds still less than half open, and that monumental mass of architectural foliage, *Helleborus corsicus*, whose big heads of lime-green flower were still like tight-clenched fists.

Strangely enough, one of the great winter beauties, *Viburnum fragrans*, was already over. Its full glory had been in October and November. But half a dozen kinds of heather had already overtaken both hellebore and cydonia: dense masses of pink, white and crimson, surely one of winter's most precious gilt-edged investments. Scattered about them were many things that I don't really count as truly winter joys: polyanthus, odd pinks and a few precocious sprigs of wallflower. But among them was at least one astonishing surprise – gold and yellow heads of gazania, miraculously untouched by frost. These belonged to the silver-leaved varieties, which I greatly prefer to the normal type.

So a morning filched from April wasn't cheating. Its joys were all genuine. What is more, they have a certain constancy that I find endearing. They are not freaks which appear only if and when the time is congenial. Except in the severest of spells, which heaven knows are always round the corner, ready to mock us and restore our climate's notorious reputation, I have rarely if ever known them to fail. And on that balmy day of light air, bird song, blue sky and gnats dancing their summer dances, I counted something like twenty-five kinds of floral stardom putting on their gracious winter act. It did the heart, the eye, the mind and the senses a great deal of good.

[22]

Some time ago two friends asked me for my advice in the matter of subjects for hedges. It was something I had never given much thought to. I have only one hedge in my garden – a forty year old *Lonicera nitida* still showing signs of prolonged war-time neglect, so that it has a certain half-drunken elephantine appearance about it. It is also so thick and woody that the top of it forms a hard platform along which a regal pair of old gentlemen pheasants used frequently to strut in all their brilliance with superb, indeed almost arrogant, dignity and pride, presenting a magnificent sight in winter, especially against snow and the brittle blue of wintry sky. Unhappily the old gentlemen have now either died of old age or have been shot.

When at last I got down to serious thought about this whole subject I had several surprises. The chief of these was the truly enormous number of subjects that may be used for hedges and their infinite variations in size, colouring, foliage and flower. I have in front of me at this moment, for instance, a catalogue listing more than a hundred different hedging subjects both evergreen and deciduous, as well as another thirty or forty varieties of roses that are also highly suited and desirable for hedges.

Of these hundred varieties no less than half are flowering hedges, which was the very thing, in fact, that my friends were looking for. In addition to this double value they also wanted a hedge, or hedges, that wouldn't block out the beauties of their Cotswold countryside and wouldn't need a 15-foot ladder when it came to the task of trimming. This, of course, is the bugbear about hedges; they can make a devil of a lot of work. In America it is the rule rather than the exception that gardens shouldn't be hedged or fenced in, but the average Englishman is Conservative about these matters and likes to have some screen between himself and his neighbours, whom he is just as likely to hate as to love.

Now clearly it is totally impossible here to list all the hedging plants, however beautiful, that may be used. I therefore propose to confine myself to just a few that are exceptional and uncommon but at the same time neither difficult nor expensive. If I were planting a new hedge what, for instance, would be my first choice? Unhesitatingly, I think, the Portugal Laurel (*Prunus lusitanica*). Evergreen, with dark bay-like leaves, handsome, well-behaved, having white flowers in June and grape-like purple berries in autumn, this excellent thing needs only light pruning to keep it in order. It is a splendid, useful aristocrat.

It is now some few years since I first saw *Eleagnus* × *ebbingei* being used as a hedge on Lake Maggiore, but I thought then, and still do, what a splendid hedge this lovely silver-green shrub, so beloved by flower arrangers, can make. Its golden-green sister, the exquisite *pungens aurea variegata*, would make an even better one. Both of these, like the Portugal Laurel, should be pruned and not clipped, into shape. I also like the form of *Prunus pissardii* called 'Blaze', with its lovely warm purple-red foliage. This can be shaped into a low hedge or allowed to develop into an informal one. Grey or silver is a desirable colour for a low hedge and nothing will provide it better than lavender, of which the variety 'Hidcote' is quite the best. But second only to it is our old and well-loved friend *Santolina* –

child's play from cuttings and easily trimmed into compact shape each spring.

Some of the berberis family make first-rate hedges and I particularly like *B. thunbergii* 'Atropurpurea Nana' from which name you will see that it is purple and dwarf. But *B. darwinii* is also excellent, a fire of brightest orange in spring. Also excellent, especially on coasts, is the sea buckthorn I mentioned in a former chapter. And what of the pittosporums? with their dainty crinkled fresh pale green foliage also so loved by flower arrangers. Long ago I was assured they were tender but two trees of mine have survived ten winters, including that of 1963 – and if a plant will survive that it will survive anything.

Roses for hedges are really too numerous to deal with in a short chapter but I confess to a secret love for that old hybrid Bourbon, 'Zéphyrine Drouhin', thornless and pink-flowered, and still a great favourite today, a hundred years after its introduction in 1873. Another unusual subject I would certainly try if I were planting a new hedge is the variegated form of *Viburnum tinus*, known to us all as Laurustinus; nor would I despise the golden variegated laurel. And hedges I wouldn't plant? Not *Lonicera nitida* again, nor on any account *Cupressus macrocarpa* which, if clipped, will surely die on you in the first severe winter. But if you do want a cupressus hedge × *Cupressocyparis leylandii* is the answer and is the fastest growing of the lot.

[23]

With the rise in popularity of flower arranging there has
been a corresponding increase in popularity of various
unusual flowers, many of which were previously scarcely
known to us in this country. Probably the most remarkable
of these is the vast and strange family of proteas. I say vast
advisedly, since Australia alone has no less than 600 species
belonging to 29 genera, most of which are not found
elsewhere and more than half of them belonging to
Western Australia alone. In South Africa there are said
to be another 100 species, many of which I am told,
alas, are in danger of extinction, thanks to the predatory
nature of tourists. It would indeed be wicked if this
were so.

As to the strangeness of the proteas the key is in the
very name itself. This comes from the mythical Greek god
Proteus, who could transform himself into any shape, and
it is an almost bewildering number of shapes that we find in
the proteas, from the globe artichoke form of many species
to others looking like large pincushions.

The proteas, though a large enough family in themselves,
have also a lot of near relatives. Probably the best known of
these and certainly one of the most beautiful is the Waratah
(botanically *Telopea speciosissima*) the national emblem of
New South Wales. This warm crimson thing is of very
protea-like shape, though if I were to describe it as very

like an incurved chrysanthemum it would probably be nearer the mark.

The grevilleas also belong to the protea family and they too are pretty numerous, being very widely distributed in Australia, where Victoria has 21 species and Western Australia 32. The bright yellow Silky oak, the largest of the family, is also a near-protea relative. The sugar bushes and Silver Trees are also related. One of the commoner sugar bushes (aptly named) is so full of honey that early settlers used to gather it and boil it up into a thick nectar for fruit preserving.

The Silver Trees are of great and delicate beauty. They are not at all unlike certain species of eucalyptus, though they are infinitely more silver. 'Grey satin' has been used to describe the leaves which cluster thickly on the upright branches and give, under the slightest breeze, a shimmering effect. Still other relatives are the genus *Leucospermum* and it is these that give the pincushion shapes. Yet another relation is the bottle-brush family, not to be confused with the well known and very attractive Australian family of that name. These bottle-brushes have the botanical name of *Mimilis*, which comes from the Greek *mimos*, a mimic.

Proteas are not only widely distributed horizontally but vertically too. One of them, *Protea vilimandscharica*, grows at a height of 9,000–11,000 feet. They also vary a good deal in stature, from a height of a foot or two to 12 or 15 feet. I have before me a picture of a large yellow-flowered bush probably some 6 or 8 feet in diameter which is of such protea-like appearance that I am astonished to find that it is, in fact, a silver tree (*Leucadendron daphnoides*). Never was there a better reason for changing its name to the Golden Tree.

Great variations in colour are also to be found in the proteas. The range goes from white to yellow and through to pink and crimson and finally, believe it or not, black.

I confess to not knowing the correct name of this black protea, but black it certainly is, so that in some ways its flower head looks more like a crouching animal or bird rather than a flower. Certainly it struck me as being more curious than beautiful, though it illustrated perfectly the strange attributes given to the family by the god Proteus.

Having lavished much praise on this vast and absorbing family it is only right to add they are not hardy in this country. I should however imagine that only a little glass protection would be enough to ensure their survival in all but the fiercest of our winters. The only drawback about this, however, is the size to which many proteas, and especially the Silver Trees, will grow. As with many near hardy things the trouble is rather like that experienced by an extremely fleshy blonde lady who is seen in an American cartoon trying to choose something new at a perfume counter. "Got anything to hold 'em back?" she is enquiring.

That certainly is the difficulty – holding 'em back. I once grew that glorious orange and scarlet beauty, *Streptosolen jamesonii*, under glass. Ravishing though it was it took such possession of the greenhouse that within two years it was a question of either it or the greenhouse. The same thing happened with a mimosa. Starting off as a mere six-inch babe in a three-inch pot it finally reared itself out of the top greenhouse lights. Delightful though it was to gather one's own mimosa in January and February the inevitable crisis came when the tree, now with a trunk of nearly a foot in diameter, had to be cut down. Even that didn't deter it and it is already on its way heavenwards again.

However, there are compensations. It is now possible to buy protea flowers, which dry beautifully and will splendidly embellish any dried-flower arrangement.

[24]

I make no apology for devoting this last chapter to a subject that has long fascinated me and of which I have written before: namely, the scent of flowers. Here, I have always felt, is an everlasting mystery: not merely the fact of scent and its infinite variations, not merely the fact that some flowers give off fragrance by day but others only at night or that some flowers have no scent at all or that from time to time a certain plant – the old-fashioned musk much loved by our Victorian and Edwardian ancestors, for example, or *Clematis montana*, all of a sudden, for no explicable reason, loses its scent and never gets it back again. It is always being said that the modern rose generally lacks the fragrance of its 19th-century ancestors, particularly the luscious hybrid perpetuals, into which you could bury your face and fancy you were drinking the perfume, like wine. If the charge that all modern roses are scentless cannot really be wholly upheld it is at least partly true and it would be interesting to know why.

But there are really three great things about the scent of flowers that fascinate and indeed puzzle me: the extraordinary effect on the senses of an inanimate something which cannot be seen, has no shape and cannot be touched or heard; its tremendous powers of evocation and association; and perhaps most remarkable of all its power to get itself recorded, visually, by the mind, which in turn will

89

preserve the image, together with some minute, even trivial, association for an entire life time.

Thus if I stand in my garden in Kent and hold a bunch of spring violets to my nostrils it isn't the immediate experience of inhaling the incomparable violet richness that gives me pleasure. The scent, in a split second, also unlocks a door, so that I am suddenly a small boy again, sitting in my grandfather's lamplit kitchen, helping to bunch violets that will be sold from his little pony-drawn market-gardener's cart on Saturday morning. I have only to put a cowslip to my nose and in a flash I am back in a Midland valley, in May, gathering cowslips with my grandmother, sixty years ago. Give me a sprig of honeysuckle and such is the evocative power of its perfume that I am instantly in a sort of sensual swoon, reliving a score of summers and all their vivid, visual associations, half a century ago.

Charles Laughton, the actor, with whom I had dinner just before he died, had a theory that the greatest of all computers was the human brain, beside which the most advanced mechanical version, for all its brilliance, was a comparative bungler. Laughton's theory is nowhere better supported than by the miracle of scent and the further miracle of the mind's ability to photograph infinite variations of it, file them away for decades and then suddenly produce, in a flash of re-experience, the correct print more swiftly than any instant camera.

Some time ago a research was instituted among artists, musicians and writers in an attempt to discover what influence scent, not only of flowers but fruit and manufactured perfumes, of earth, of rain on summer dust, of sea-weed, new-mown hay, leather, cloth, a girl's hair, a sea-salt wind and countless other sources, had on them. The results are too varied and complex to go into here but over and over again these highly sensitized people confessed to the great stimulant power that various scents, and some of them very unlikely ones, had on them mentally, sensuously and creatively. Some even went so far as to admit that without the stimulus of some scent of a powerful association – lily-of-the-valley was one, lime-flowers another, clove carnations another – their creative juices wouldn't even begin to flow. On me the scent of honey-suckle has much the same effect. One swift draught of that essence of summer sets all my creative senses dancing.

If the power of scent is so great on those of us still blessed with the gift of sight how much more magnified it must be on those unfortunate enough no longer to possess it. Laughton's theory of the marvels of the human computer may have to be extended to include another, namely that scent is itself a sort of second sight. Thus all scent, to the blind, must be infinitely precious. The element that cannot be touched, seen or heard has its own tremendous power of visual creation.

A foot treading on a bed of thyme, a salvia leaf rolled between thumb and forefinger, young grass bruised by summer feet, a pot of rose petals, the strong odour of dying oak leaves in autumn woods as your feet brush through them – it would be sad indeed if we who still have sight took these things, seemingly trivial though they are, for granted. I will certainly see that I don't in future. In fact I will go about my garden looking for scent and when I don't find it I will plant some. Then perhaps, in the next century, one of my grandchildren, chancing on that most heavily perfumed of all pinks, *Dianthus* 'Loveliness' (try it, it is a wholly exquisite thing) will take the swiftest breath of it and be most miraculously transported back to another world.

40-26